HIS GLORY
REVEALED

HIS GLORY REVEALED

A Devotional

JOHN HAGEE

THOMAS NELSON PUBLISHERS
Nashville

Published in Nashville, Tennessee, by Thomas Nelson, Inc., Publishers.

Scripture quotations noted NKJV are from THE NEW KING JAMES VERSION. Copyright © 1979, 1980, 1982, 1990, Thomas Nelson, Inc., Publishers.

Scripture quotations noted KJV are from the KING JAMES VERSION.

Scripture quotations noted NIV are from the HOLY BIBLE: NEW INTERNATIONAL VERSION Æ. Copyright © 1973, 1978, 1984 by International Bible Society. Used by permission of Zondervan Publishing House. All rights reserved.

Library of Congress Cataloging–in–Publication Data

Hagee, John C.
    His glory revealed: a devotional / John Hagee.
       p. cm.
    ISBN 0-7852-6965-7
    1. Fasts and feasts in the Bible—Typology—Meditations. 2. Fasts and feasts—Judaism—Meditations. I. Title
BS680.F37H34 1999
263'.9—dc21
                                98–49635
                                  CIP

Printed in the United States of America.
1 2 3 4 5 6 QPK 04 03 02 01 00 99

DEDICATION

*Dedicated to America's finest congregation at
Cornerstone Church, whose unfailing love and loyalty
has helped me preach the Gospel of Jesus Christ
without apology for 32 years.*

CONTENTS

Part Two: Feasts of the Latter Rain

His Glory Revealed
Understanding the Seven
Feasts of the Lord

*A*s the pastor of Cornerstone Church and a teacher of prophecy on national television, people are always asking me about signs of the end times. They are asking:

- "How long do we have before the Rapture?"
- "Will the church go through the Tribulation?"
- "Are we about to have a worldwide economic crash?"
- "Who is the coming Antichrist?"
- "Why will there be a holy war over the city of Jerusalem?"

The answers are contained in this simple principle: *The God who created the heavens operates in sevens.* Seven is God's number of perfection and/or completion.

- There are seven days in the week.
- There are many sevens mentioned in Scripture: Jacob served Laban seven years, there are seven branches of the golden candlestick, seven trumpets and seven priests,

seven days of siege upon Jericho, seven churches, seven spirits, and seven stars.

- There are seven ages and dispensations from Genesis 1:1 to the conclusion of the book of Revelation.
- There are seven seals, seven trumpets, and seven vials in the Tribulation (the first forty-two months) and the Great Tribulation (the latter forty-two months) of seven years of hell on earth.

If you want to understand what God will do in the future, look to what He has done in the past. God does not want you to live in ignorance; He has always wanted His people to understand His actions. When God decided to destroy Sodom and Gomorrah, He decided to warn Abraham: "Shall I hide from Abraham what I am doing . . . ?" He asked (Gen. 18:17 NKJV). One-quarter of the Bible was prophetic at the time it was written, not because God wanted to confuse His people, but because He wants us to be filled with understanding about the future!

God has ordained seven portals through which we can glimpse His divine plan, and these are the seven feasts of Israel. "Speak to the children of Israel," the Lord told Moses, "and say to them: 'The feasts of the LORD, which you shall proclaim to be holy convocations, these are My feasts'" (Lev. 23:2 NKJV).

The Lord Himself established seven festivals to guide Israel through the centuries until the Messiah comes. Christians often falsely assume these feasts are exclusively for Jewish people, but the Bible makes it clear that these days belong to the Lord. Everyone, Jew and Gentile, has the right to draw near.

These seven feasts have several purposes: First, they are intended to draw the minds and hearts of the people toward God. Second, they are a time of sweet communion and joy.

Finally, they illustrate profound spiritual truths and create a picture of God's plan for the ages.

Just as seven days finish a weekly cycle, these seven festivals portray the work of God on earth. Though modern Jews have added other holidays and festive occasions to their religious calendar, the seven feasts we will study in this book were designed and established by God Himself in the twenty-third chapter of Leviticus. Through these festivals, God is giving us a snapshot of what He has already done, as well as a prophetic portrait of what is to come in the years ahead.

The Hebrew word for "feast," *mo'ed*, means "a set or appointed time." Of very similar meaning is *mikrah*, indicating "a rehearsal or recital." Each feast, like a dress rehearsal, offers a significant portrait of part of God's prophetic plan. The combined seven feasts, divinely instituted shortly after the people of Israel had left the slavery of Egypt, would be a spiritual blueprint of what lies ahead for Israel, Jerusalem, and the rest of the world.

This devotional book will take you through seven weeks, with one study for each of five days. These daily readings will help you understand not only the meaning of each of the seven feasts, but the prophetic significance of each festival. I believe you will also come to appreciate the incredible complexity and majestic simplicity of God's divine seven-thousand-year plan for mankind.

As we study each holiday and its place in the Jewish year, we will be walking on God's timeline that stretches from Eden to eternity. While we cannot know the day or the hour of Jesus Christ's return to earth, we can reflect on the possible month for both the Rapture and the Second Coming. The month is revealed in the accumulative meaning of the seven feasts.

As we begin our study, remember this basic principle: Everything God will do, He has already done. "Surely the Lord

GOD does nothing unless He reveals His secret to His servants the prophets" (Amos 3:7 NKJV).

Stepping-Stones to Splendor

Through these seven festivals, God reveals His seven-thousand-year plan for humanity. The Bible says, "But, beloved, do not forget this one thing, that with the Lord one day is as a thousand years, and a thousand years as one day" (2 Peter 3:8 NKJV). And the psalmist wrote, "For a thousand years in Your sight are like yesterday when it is past" (Ps. 90:4 NKJV).

Do you see? Every one of the seven feasts represents one of God's millennial moments. God has given us pictures, both in a simple seven-day week and in the seven festivals, of His plan for the future. Just as God commands us to rest on the Sabbath after six days, we will enter into rest after six thousand years in a one-thousand-year time span known as the Millennium. The world as we know it will end!

We'll trade this politically correct madhouse for the paradise of God. We will leave this hedonistic, materialistic, and neopagan cesspool for the throne room of God's perfect Lamb.

A word about calendars: In order to fully appreciate the meaning of the Jewish festivals, you must understand the Jewish calendar. First, for obvious reasons, the Jewish calendar does not count years since the birth of Christ. In biblical times, years were identified according to historical happenings—i.e., "in the year King Uzziah died." The Jewish tradition of counting years since the creation of the world began in talmudic times and was adopted as *the* definitive Jewish method of dating after the Christian calendar came into existence. (The year of this book's publication, 1999, falls in years 5759–60 on the Jewish calendar.)

The defining month of the Jewish year is Abib (late March or

April on the English calendar) and was designated by God Himself in Deuteronomy 16:1: "Observe the month of Abib, and keep the Passover to the LORD your God, for in the month of Abib the LORD your God brought you out of Egypt by night." Abib must fall in the springtime, and occasionally, when spring came late, ancient rabbis added a second month in order to facilitate the observance of Passover and set the dates for all other festivals. In order to reconcile the lunar calendar to the solar year, every nineteen years a second month of Adar must be added in seven different "leap years."

Over the centuries, the names of the months have changed. Ancient names such as *Abib* and *Ziv* have given way to the traditional month names of *Nisan, Iyar, Sivan, Tamuz, Av, Elul, Tishri, Chesvan, Kislev, Tevet, Shevat,* and *Adar.* Therefore, Passover now occurs in the Jewish month of Nisan.

A Jewish day has twenty-four hours and begins in the evening, at sunset: "So the evening and the morning were the first day" (Gen. 1:5 NKJV).

> *And* you shall rejoice in your feast, you and your son and your daughter, your male servant and your female servant and the Levite, the stranger and the fatherless and the widow, who are within your gates.
> —DEUTERONOMY 16:14 NKJV

Before the advent of calendars and clocks, the people of Israel lived by the unchanging calendar of the seasons. The first four festivals—the Feast of Passover, the Feast of Unleavened Bread, the Feast of Firstfruits, and the Feast of Pentecost—take us from the beginning of spring to the gathering of the wheat harvest. The three fall festivals—the Feast of Trumpets, the Feast of

Atonement, and the Feast of Tabernacles—remind the Jewish people that winter lies ahead.

The two sets of holidays also coincide with the two annual seasons of rain. Spring brings the former rain; the latter rain comes in the fall. The prophet Hosea knew the seasons and rain cycles were a clear picture of things to come. Inspired by the Holy Spirit, he wrote of the Messiah, saying, "He will come to us like the rain, like the latter and former rain to the earth" (Hos. 6:3 NKJV).

Hosea meant that Jesus Christ, the Messiah, would come twice—once in the former rain, and again in the latter. The four feasts of the former rain, Passover, Unleavened Bread, Firstfruits, and Pentecost, are acts one through four in God's preparation for the divine drama of the Second Coming. The prophetic fulfillment of those feasts lies behind us. But the hands on God's clock are moving swiftly. As the first four feasts predicted what now lies in history, so the next three festivals will help us calculate what lies ahead.

It is my hope and prayer that you will use this book thoughtfully and with a prayerful heart. Take time to pencil in your thoughts, read the Scriptures, consider carefully what the prophets are saying. And then, when you have completed this seven-week devotional, I pray that you will live in joy and absolute confidence, with an eye to the future and an appreciation for the past.

God does not want us to live in ignorance, defeat, or misery. He designed His festivals to strengthen weary hearts, comfort lost souls, and bring truth to a dying world. Set aside some quiet time each day to come with me as we explore the rich tapestry of meaning behind the seven feasts of the Lord.

The Feasts of the Former Rain

PART

One

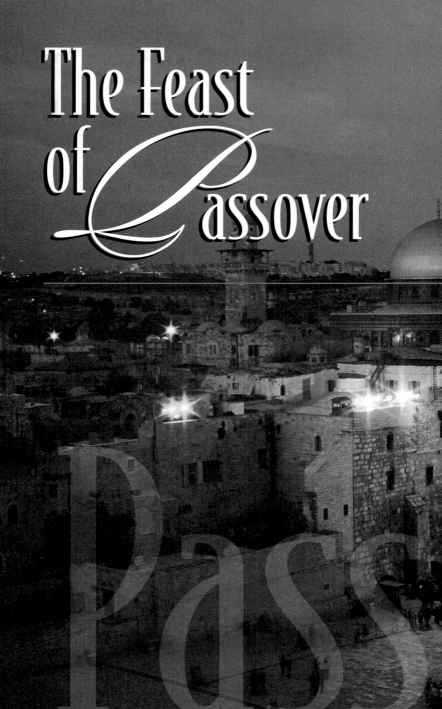

The Feast
of Passover

SEPTEMBER 25–
OCTOBER 1
1999

OCTOBER 14-20
2000

OCTOBER 2-8
2001

SEPTEMBER 21-27
2002

OCTOBER 11-17
2003

SEPTEMBER 30–
OCTOBER 6
2004

OCTOBER 18-24
2005

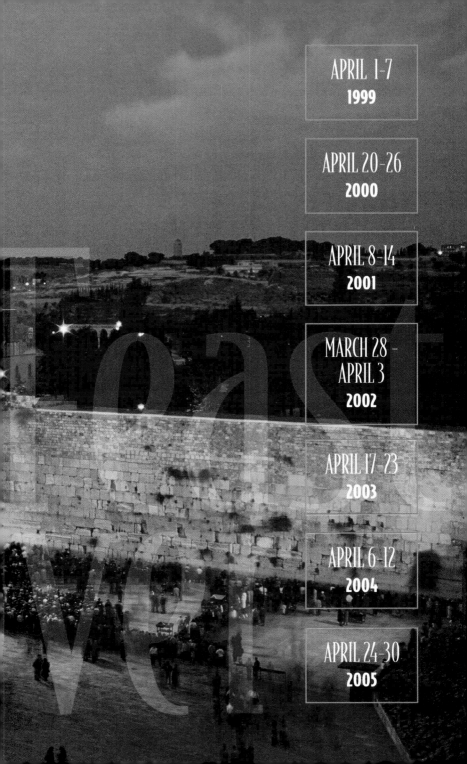

APRIL 1-7
1999

APRIL 20-26
2000

APRIL 8-14
2001

MARCH 28 –
APRIL 3
2002

APRIL 17-23
2003

APRIL 6-12
2004

APRIL 24-30
2005

Day One: The Feast of Passover

*B*efore we can begin an in-depth study of the Jewish feasts and their application to our lives, we need to examine the Scriptures through which God established these festivals.

> These are the feasts of the LORD, holy convocations which you shall proclaim at their appointed times. On the fourteenth day of the first month at twilight is the LORD's Passover. (Lev. 23:4–5 NKJV)

> Now the LORD spoke to Moses and Aaron in the land of Egypt, saying, "This month shall be your beginning of months; it shall be the first month of the year to you. Speak to all the congregation of Israel, saying: 'On the tenth of this month every man shall take for himself a lamb, according to the house of his father, a lamb for a household. And if the household is too small for the lamb, let him and his neighbor next to his house take it according to the number of the persons; according to each man's need you shall make your count for the lamb.
> 'Your lamb shall be without blemish, a male of the first year. You may take it from the sheep or from the goats. Now you shall keep it until the fourteenth day of the same month. Then the whole assembly of the congregation of Israel shall kill it at twilight. And they shall take some of the blood and put it on the two doorposts and on the lintel of the houses where they eat it. Then they shall eat the flesh on that night;

roasted in fire, with unleavened bread and with bitter herbs they shall eat it. Do not eat it raw, nor boiled at all with water, but roasted in fire—its head with its legs and its entrails. You shall let none of it remain until morning, and what remains of it until morning you shall burn with fire . .

'So this day shall be to you a memorial; and you shall keep it as a feast to the LORD throughout your generations. You shall keep it as a feast by an everlasting ordinance.'" (Ex. 12:1–10, 14 NKJV).

If you think back to just about any significant or memorable event in your life, chances are good there was a meal involved. In the Bible, breaking bread together was considered a bond of loyalty between two or more people. It was considered unthinkable in Bible times to eat at a man's table and then do or say anything to his hurt. This is the basis of King David's shock when he wrote, "Even my own familiar friend in whom I trusted, Who ate my bread, Has lifted up his heel against me" (Ps. 41:9 NKJV).

When Judas Iscariot ate the Passover meal with Jesus and then sold Him for thirty pieces of silver, he became the ultimate traitor of all history.

When the bride of Christ is raptured, we will sit down at the marriage supper and take the holy Communion expressing our love and loyalty forever to King Jesus.

That's one reason God designed Passover as a meal. This hurried supper was a memorable part of God's wonderful deliverance of His people from Egyptian bondage.

Consider Egypt, scene of the first Passover. That wealthy, fertile black land was the envy of the world. The Egyptians built pyramids we study and admire even to this day, but the

pharaoh of the Exodus enslaved and burdened the children of Abraham, drowning their sons in the Nile and attempting to crush the Israelites' spirit with hard labor.

But God heard His people's cries for redemption, and He sent Moses to deliver them from slavery. As the Hebrews watched nine plagues stupefy and stun their Egyptian taskmasters, they heard Moses' words of warning and scrambled to obey. God would send His death angel over the land of Egypt, and any house not marked by lamb's blood would suffer the loss of its firstborn.

The Jews obeyed. They killed the sacrificial lamb, roasted it whole, and ate fully dressed, many standing at the table. Doubtless they heard the Egyptians' keening wails of mourning even as they ate. And they realized God had delivered them even before the sun arose:

> So Pharaoh rose in the night, he, all his servants, and all the Egyptians; and there was a great cry in Egypt, for there was not a house where there was not one dead.
>
> Then [Pharaoh] called for Moses and Aaron by night, and said, "Rise, go out from among my people, both you and the children of Israel. And go, serve the LORD as you have said. Also take your flocks and your herds, as you have said, and be gone; and bless me also."
>
> And the Egyptians urged the people, that they might send them out of the land in haste. For they said, "We shall all be dead."
>
> So the people took their dough before it was leavened, having their kneading bowls bound up in their clothes on their shoulders. Now the children of Israel had done according to the word of Moses, and they had asked from the Egyptians articles of silver, articles of gold, and clothing.

And the LORD had given the people favor in the sight of the Egyptians, so that they granted them what they requested. Thus they plundered the Egyptians. (Ex. 12:30–36 NKJV)

There is a postscript to the story: As the Hebrews made their way back to Canaan, back to the land God had promised Abraham and his descendants by blood covenant (Gen. 15), Pharaoh changed his mind and set out in hot pursuit with six hundred choice chariots. At the Red Sea he caught up with the multitude of Israelites, and gaped in awe to see them walking across a dry seabed. Emboldened by his own arrogance, he tried to follow, but the walls of the Red Sea came crashing down upon him. In the end, Pharaoh's mighty army was consumed by God's wrath. Pharaoh himself was soon floating faceup, grotesquely bloated in the heat of Egypt's sun, his sightless eyes staring at God, whom he could not see and whom he would never know. His arrogant query to Moses, "Who is the Lord, that I should obey Him?" received a divine response. In one hour, the most powerful man on earth was reduced to fish food!

Father, how blessed we are to be called Your children! We can say, "Behold, this is our God; We have waited for Him, and He will save us. This is the LORD; We have waited for Him; We will be glad and rejoice in His salvation" (Isa. 25:9 NKJV). There is no God like our God!

Day Two: Passover in the Time of Christ

*J*erusalem was a crowded city during the days of Passover. The city's usual population of one hundred thousand was more than doubled by religious pilgrims who came to visit the Temple at Passover. Every inn was filled to capacity, every home brimmed with guests, and many pilgrims set up tents and shelters against the city wall and in the open places. Yet everyone found a place—and that simple fact was counted as a Passover miracle.

Not all the travelers were holy pilgrims. Merchants came from far and near, eager to sell assorted wares and the many animals that would be needed for sacrifices. The Roman procurator also arrived from Caesarea, with additional soldiers to guard against a possible uprising of a discontented and oppressed people.

Jews and Jewish converts from all over the world filled the city with colorful garments and a cacophony of noise. Merchants dickered over the price of animals in every imaginable language, housewives bartered for spices with which they would prepare the Passover meal. The heads of households searched for relatives and friends to join them at dinner, for the Passover lamb must be eaten in one night, with nothing reserved for the morrow. Since one family could not eat an entire lamb, groups of at least ten arranged to dine together. Because some groups became very large, and any one individual might receive only a small taste of the sacrificial lamb, an additional secondary sacrifice, or *chagigah*, was introduced.

Unlike the Paschal lamb, the *chagigah* did not have to be completely eaten before dawn.

Throughout the activity and confusion, Passover was a time of rejoicing, an occasion to remember the past, hope for the future, and renew old acquaintances.

The morning before Passover, thousands of priests and Levites from all over Judea gathered in the Temple. By midday, everyone from tailors to shoemakers to housewives had ceased from their work. Thousands of Jews began to stream through the town, each head of household leading the family's sacrificial lamb. By three o'clock, the priests had assembled in the Temple courtyard, ready to begin sacrificing the Passover lambs.

When the Temple's outer court had filled, Temple guards closed the gates temporarily. The Levites blew the ceremonial threefold blast on their trumpets (*shofroth*) and the sacrifices began. The head of each household slew his animal, the lamb that had been purchased four days before and kept tied beside the house like a beloved family pet. Behind him, the priests stood in rows, some with silver bowls to catch the blood, others singing psalms of praise.

The huge crowds required that the gates be opened and closed three times so

every family had a chance to offer its sacrifice. The ceremony and ritual were dignified and reverent, and when each family left, the father carrying the slaughtered animal over his shoulder, all hearts expectantly waited to experience the holy awe found in this night of redemption.

That afternoon, the scents of roasting lamb wafted over the city in a great wave. Homes grew noisy as guests began arriving, and all were made welcome. At last, when all preparations were complete, the head of the family sat at the head of the table and led the ceremonial observance of the Passover meal. First, a glass of wine was taken, then the right hand washed while everyone partook of lettuce dipped in a tart liquid. Then the sacrificial lamb was served, eaten with unleavened bread and bitter herbs dipped in charoset, a mixture of ground nuts and fruits soaked in wine. After this the second part of the ceremonial evening began—the reciting of the story of Passover, and the discussion of the rituals that accompany it. The eldest son of the household asked, "Why is this night different from all other nights?" and his father answered with excerpts from the Bible explaining the Hebrews' miraculous deliverance from Egypt. When he began to sing Hallel (Pss. 115–18), all the guests joined in. The feast concluded with a prayer for redemption.

What I've just described was the general pattern of Passover during the time of Jesus Christ. Now I'd like you to look at one particular Passover—the fourteenth day of Abib, A.D. 33. The Levites have just opened the doors of the Temple so that the crowds can enter to offer their sacrificial lambs. At the exact moment each head of household takes a knife and prepares to slaughter the lamb that must be sacrificed for his family, Jesus is hanging on a cross outside the city, deserted by all but a few followers and the Roman executioners.

The sky darkens, and the crowds inside the Temple grow silent and pensive. While the stones of the Temple courtyard run red with the blood of lambs and goats, the Lamb of God spills His life's blood outside the city. While the father in each household slaughters a lamb for the sake of his family, God the Father slaughters His holy Lamb for the sake of all who would accept Christ's gift of forgiveness and eternal life.

What wondrous love! What amazing grace!

Never forget it . . . your redemption was purchased by the precious blood of the Lamb of God.

Father, how grateful we are that You loved us enough to send Your Only begotten Son as a spotless Passover Lamb. We know that without the shedding of blood there is no remission of sin, and only Your spotless sacrifice could ever wash our sins away. Thank You for the blood of Your Son.

DAY THREE: PRESENT-DAY PASSOVER

> *In* each generation, every person is obliged to feel as though he or she personally came out of Egypt.
> —*THE PASSOVER* HAGGADAH

After the destruction of the Temple in A.D. 70, the custom of making a Passover sacrifice disappeared. The Passover celebration took place entirely in the home, and though the family did eat roasted meat and a roasted egg (to represent the *chagigah*), the sacrificial lamb disappeared, for it could be sacrificed only in Jerusalem. The Passover festival itself has been absorbed into the Festival of Unleavened Bread, which we'll discuss next week.

With the element of sacrifice and blood missing, what remains? Modern Jews consider Passover, or Pesach, a symbol and ceremony of liberation.

> The liberation of the Jewish people from Egyptian bondage has become a powerful symbol of redemption—not only the redemption of the Jewish people but the redemption of the entire world. The *Haggadah* [the tale of the Exodus from Egypt read on Passover night] . . . recognizes that slavery is not limited to physical bondage, but that spiritual slavery and social degradation are no less potent methods of depriving human beings of liberty.[1]

Yes, my friends, Passover does mean liberation for the entire world—liberation from sin and death! When Jesus sacrificially gave His life on the cross, He became the Passover Lamb who bought forgiveness for any who are willing to accept it.

Passover is Israel's great celebration of freedom. It is a matter of historical fact that the Hebrews were owned by Pharaoh, not by Egypt. That unyielding tyrant cared nothing for God or man. Believing he was a god on earth, his foolish arrogance hung around his neck like a millstone, finally sending him to his death in the depths of the Red Sea. When Pharaoh drowned, his death canceled his control over the slaves. His ownership of the Jews ended instantly and permanently.

Every year when Passover comes, God reminds His people—Jews and Gentiles—that He is the only One who can set them free. You and I are sinners, but God's gift of forgiveness is offered to anyone who will accept it. Acceptance is more than an emotion or an intellectual understanding—it's a commitment of the will. If you have willfully surrendered your life to Christ, you have been "sealed" with the blood of the Passover Lamb. Death and sin no longer have any claim upon you. You are free!

You and I were once slaves to Satan and sin. We lived in chains, in bondage to fear. When Jesus Christ surrendered Himself to become our

Passover Lamb, He ended the reign of death in our lives. The Lamb of God shouted from the cross, "It is finished!" and at that moment we were liberated from death, hell, and the grave. We have been freed from the guilt of the past and the fear of tomorrow. Satan is forever a defeated foe. "Therefore," wrote the apostle John, "if the Son makes you free, you shall be free indeed" (John 8:36 NKJV).

> The Jewish Midrash teaches that just as the Red Sea did not split until the Israelites stepped into it, so redemption cannot come unless we take the first step.

You need no longer be defeated by yesterday. There is no need for you to be afraid of tomorrow. God does not say, "I am the Great I WAS." Nor does He say, "I am the Great I WILL BE." You can live in joy and victory today for God declares, "I AM [the Great] I AM" (Ex. 3:14 NKJV). He's the God of the present. He is the Great Liberator.

Father, we're so thankful that You have set us free. As our Passover Lamb, You broke the chains that held us fast to a lifetime of sin and an eternity of darkness. Forgive us when we dredge up the failings of the past. We are born again in You.

Day Four: The Prophecy of Passover

*J*esus fulfilled the meaning of the Passover ritual. The moment John the Baptist saw Jesus, he exclaimed, "Behold! The Lamb of God who takes away the sin of the world!" (John 1:29 NKJV). Jesus was God's male Lamb, without spot or blemish. He was examined by the chief priests and elders, Pilate, Herod, the high priest, and even the repentant thief on the cross. All who examined Him found Him blameless.

Pilate, the Roman procurator, cried out, "I find no fault in Him" (John 19:6 NKJV). And just as the Passover lamb was put on public display for four days, Jesus stood before Israel in the Temple for the four days prior to Passover and was examined by the Pharisees. He was God's final, perfect offering to end the reign of sin and death over humanity.

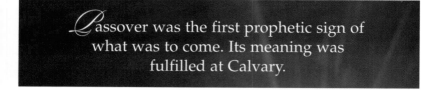

*P*assover was the first prophetic sign of what was to come. Its meaning was fulfilled at Calvary.

The Jewish scholar Hayyim Schauss, writing in *The Jewish Festivals,* says that Passover, or Pesach, had reached a pinnacle of importance during the time of Christ. Jerusalem lay under the heavy hand of the Romans at that time, and, according to Schauss, "During this period the Messianic hope flamed up, and in the minds of the Jews the deliverance of the future became bound up with the first redemption in Jewish history:

the deliverance from Egypt . . . This belief gained added strength in this period of Roman occupation and oppression. Jews began to believe that the Messiah would be a second Moses and would free the Jews the self-same eve, the eve of Pesach.[2]

The four days in which God commanded the Israelites to put the lamb on display also have eschatological significance. The Jews believed that the Messiah would come four thousand years after the creation of Adam as part of God's seven-thousand-year-plan to redeem fallen man and restore the world to the condition of Eden's innocence.[3]

Israel was looking for a redeemer on a white horse as a mighty conqueror to crush Roman oppression. God sent Jesus as a baby in a manger. The past was the guide to the future. The Passover forever declared that God saves His people through the shedding of blood.

As the hands of God's prophetic stopwatch sweep past each hour of every passing day, His people know they can look to the future without fear or apprehension. We have assurance of what cannot yet be measured. Jesus, our Passover Lamb, will yet appear a second time.

In his vision of the end times chronicled in Revelation 5, John the Revelator looked upon heaven's throne room. God held a scroll sealed with seven seals, and a strong angel proclaimed, "Who is worthy to open the scroll and loose its seals?" (v. 2 NKJV).

No one in heaven or on the earth or under the earth was able to open the scroll or even look at it, and John wept. But then one of the elders said to him, "Behold, the Lion of the tribe of Judah, the Root of David, has prevailed to open the scroll and to loose its seven seals" (v. 5 NKJV).

And John looked, and in the midst of the throne and the

four living creatures and the elders stood a Lamb as though it had been slain. And He came and took the scroll. And when He had taken it, the heavenly attendants fell down before the Lamb, and they sang a new song, saying, "You are worthy to take the scroll, and to open its seals; for You were slain, and have redeemed us to God by Your blood out of every tribe and tongue and people and nation. And have made us kings and priests to our God; and we shall reign on the earth" (vv. 9–10 NKJV).

Their song grew as others joined in, ten thousand times ten thousand, and thousands of thousands saying with a loud voice, "Worthy is the Lamb who was slain to receive power and riches and wisdom, and strength and honor and glory and blessing!" (v. 12 NKJV).

Ah, my friends. We talk about the fact that one day every knee will bow before Jesus, but I wonder if we have any conception of how powerful that moment will be. Every creature, mortal and immortal, weak and powerful, godly and ungodly, will bow before the Passover Lamb.

He is the seed of the woman who crushed the head of the serpent! (Gen. 3:15).

He is worthy of our love and devotion and worship.

He is worthy of power, and glory, and honor.

Father, I have so little to give, for all I hold dear comes from You. But Your Son, Your Passover Lamb, deserves my highest praise and adoration.
Worthy is the Lamb!

Day Five: Passover Made Personal

*I*f you want to know more about things to come, consider the story of Joseph, the beloved son of Jacob. He is a mirror of the Messiah.

Joseph was betrayed by his vengeful, jealous brothers who planned his death but eventually sold him into slavery in Egypt. He suffered among people who were not of his heritage, and after many years of slavery and imprisonment, he was elevated to the second highest position in the land. He was exalted to the right hand of the king, given a name at which every knee had to bow, and presented with a Gentile bride. His brothers, driven by the gnawing pain of hunger, ventured into Egypt and stood before Joseph three times, never recognizing the truth until he revealed his identity. When Joseph revealed himself to his brothers, they fell on one another's necks and wept openly.

The Jewish people, sons of Abraham, have now returned to the land of Israel three times. The first time was when they returned from Egypt under the direction of Moses. The second time they returned from captivity with Nehemiah to rebuild the wall around Jerusalem. In 1948 they reclaimed their ancestral title to the land for the third time. One day soon, He will reveal Himself and they will recognize their Brother.

Joseph told the sons of Jacob, "I am your brother whom you rejected, but I have been exalted" (see Gen. 45).

The first time Messiah came He was a baby in a manger, surrounded by donkeys and goats. The next time He comes

He will be mounted on a milk-white stallion thundering through the clouds of heaven with the armies of God following Him. On His head will be many crowns, for He will come back to earth as King of kings and Lord of lords.

The first time Jesus came He was brought before Pilate; He was dragged before Herod. He was mocked, spit upon, and forced to wear a scarlet robe of mockery. The next time He comes, Pilate shall be brought before Him. Herod will be dragged before Him. Hitler will be hauled before Him, and that infamous hater of the Jewish people will bow before the King of the Jews and confess that He is Lord to the glory of God the Father.

The first time the Lamb of God came He was nailed to a bitter rugged cross where He suffered and bled and died alone. The next time He comes He will put His foot on the Mount of Olives and it shall split in half. He will walk across the Kidron Valley and through the eastern gate and set His throne up on the Temple mount. From there He shall reign for one thousand years in the Millennium. Following that will be the Great White Throne Judgment, after which human time shall cease and eternity will begin.

Knowing what is to come, let us hold fast to our faith without wavering, for He who promised to remain with us is faithful. Let me challenge you to make Passover real in your life every day. During the

Christmas holidays we often speak of keeping Christmas every day of the year, but how much more precious is Passover! Without the Lamb of God's supreme sacrifice, we would be lost for eternity!

Our generation has grown too sophisticated to talk about the precious blood of Jesus. Modern hymnals avoid the old hymns like "Power in the Blood" and "There Is a Fountain," but, my friend, this truth remains—without the shedding of Jesus' blood, we would have no hope of salvation. Paul wrote that in Jesus "we have redemption through His blood" (Eph. 1:7 NKJV), and we who were once far off "have been brought near by the blood of Christ" (Eph. 2:13 NKJV).

I will never be shy about claiming the blood of Jesus Christ, for it alone has the power to save a sinner in the hour of judgment. The blood shed for me on Calvary was from God's spotless Passover Lamb, and the angel of destruction can never touch me. Hallelujah!

There is a fountain filled with blood
Drawn from Emmanuel's veins,
And sinners, plunged beneath that flood,
Lose all their guilty stains.
The dying thief rejoiced to see
That fountain in his day;
And there may I, though vile as he,
Wash all my sins away . . .[4]
—William Cowper

The Feast
Of Unleavened
Bread

APRIL 1-7
1999

APRIL 20-26
2000

APRIL 8-14
2001

MARCH 28 –
APRIL 3
2002

APRIL 17-23
2003

APRIL 6-12
2004

APRIL 24-30
2005

Day One: The Feast of Unleavened Bread

*T*hree feasts—Unleavened Bread, Pentecost, and Tabernacles—are often called the pilgrimage festivals, for families were expected to travel to the Temple in order to make the appropriate sacrifices. "Three times a year," God commanded Moses, "all your males shall appear before the LORD your God in the place which He chooses: at the Feast of Unleavened Bread, at the Feast of Weeks, and at the Feast of Tabernacles; and they shall not appear before the LORD empty-handed" (Deut. 16:16 NKJV).

These were, in part, festivals of thanksgiving to celebrate the bountiful barley, wheat, and grape harvests. But God did not intend for these celebrations to mirror the harvest festivals of the heathen Canaanites. He deliberately linked the harvest festivals with religious rituals so the Jews would remember His mighty deliverance and provision for them. In addition, He promised that their lands would never be attacked by an enemy so long as they celebrated the pilgrimage festivals according to His command. "For I will cast out the nations before you and enlarge your borders; neither will any man covet your land when you go up to appear before the LORD your God three times in the year" (Ex. 34:24 NKJV).

As the years passed, Passover and the Feast of Unleavened Bread merged into one observance. We've already studied Passover. Now let's take a look at the Scriptures concerning the second festival, the Feast of Unleavened Bread.

So this day shall be to you a memorial; and you shall keep it as a feast to the LORD throughout your generations. You shall keep it as a feast by an everlasting ordinance. Seven days you shall eat unleavened bread. On the first day you shall remove leaven from your houses. For whoever eats leavened bread from the first day until the seventh day, that person shall be cut off from Israel.

On the first day there shall be a holy convocation, and on the seventh day there shall be a holy convocation for you. No manner of work shall be done on them; but that which everyone must eat—that only may be prepared by you. So you shall observe the Feast of Unleavened Bread, for on this same day I will have brought your armies out of the land of Egypt. Therefore you shall observe this day throughout your generations as an everlasting ordinance. (Ex. 12:14–17 NKJV)

At evening on the fourteenth day of the month, after the sacrifice of the Passover lamb, God told the Hebrews to eat unleavened bread. Because the fifteenth day began at sunset, the people were actually eating the sacrificial lamb and unleavened bread at the Passover meal—which today is referred to as the seder.

The heavenly Father decreed that any Jew eating leavened bread (made with yeast) during this period should be cut off from the people. Why was His judgment so strong? Because in the Bible, Old Testament and New Testament, *leaven* is a metaphor for *sin*. Leaven represents the pride and arrogance that lead men to feel they have no need of God. The Bible says, "God resists the proud . . ." (James 4:6 NKJV) and "These six things the LORD hates . . . a proud look" (Prov. 6:16–17 NKJV).

- Pride was Nebuchadnezzar surveying his kingdom and saying, "Look what I've done." The result of pride was Nebuchadnezzar on his hands and knees eating grass in a cow pasture.
- Pride is an acid that turns the finest fruit bitter.
- Pride is a shallow and superficial weed that grows in all soils, without need of water or care. It consumes and destroys every living thing it overshadows.
- Pride is a swelling of the heart filled with ego and self-importance. Pride raises you above others until you look down on them.
- Pride is the basis of racism that divides the church and America. There is no white church, black church, brown church, or yellow church in Scripture. There is only the blood-bought church of Jesus Christ.
- Pride is a cancer that rots the soul. A man infected with pride needs nothing . . . not even God!

Picture a scene with me, if you will: Imagine a Hebrew participating in the Exodus. He has watched the hand of God peel back the edges of the Red Sea so His people could walk across on dry ground; he has seen Pharaoh and his army drowned as the waters crashed back to their rightful place. Our Hebrew traveler has watched God bring water from a rock; he has followed the pillar of cloud by day and been comforted by the sight of the pillar of fire by night. Moreover, he has heard Moses explicitly state—on several occasions—that the God of Abraham, Isaac, and Jacob has commanded that leaven shall be put away during the Feast of Unleavened Bread.

What if our imaginary Hebrew decides to have a nice little yeast roll for lunch? What does his rebellious action suggest?

By today's standards of gross immorality, eating leavened bread during this festival week would be considered laughably unimportant. Yet God commanded that any person who ate leavened bread during this feast should be stoned to death. Think of it! What's God saying here? He's saying He has zero tolerance for sin!

This is a message America has forgotten. We have become a nation of drugs, divorce, drunkenness, abortion, pornography, incest, and homosexuality. We are lovers of pleasure rather than lovers of God. We snap our fingers at God as if He were a cosmic bellhop.

But God never changes!

God has always poured out His wrath on people and nations who refuse to confess their sin. If our country does not have a time of national repentance, America will experience the wrath of God on her economy, on her land's ability to grow food through floods and scorching heat, and on her children, who will continue to march into captivity to drugs, gangs, sexual diseases, and satanism. "Blessed is the nation whose God is the LORD" (Ps. 33:12 NKJV)—that verse does *not* describe America.

> *Why* does God hate sin? Because sin is man's declaration of independence of God.

The rebellious Hebrew traveler who snacks on a yeast roll during the Feast of Unleavened Bread is breaking a clear command of God. He is saying that he doesn't care about God's law. He's indicating that he considers himself above God's law, and that God's will doesn't matter. He is literally thumbing his nose at the God who brought him out of Egypt.

Hear me! You don't break God's law . . . God's law will break you.

Such arrogance is hard to imagine, yet it exists all around us, just as it flourished even among the religious leaders in Christ's time. Jesus said, "Take heed and beware of the leaven of the Pharisees and the Sadducees" (Matt. 16:6 NKJV). This sort of arrogance exists in the church; it's contagious and it's cancerous. Just like yeast, sin puffs us up. Paul felt led to warn the early church, "Your glorying is not good. Do you not know that a little leaven leavens the whole lump?" (1 Cor. 5:6 NKJV). His point? A "little" pride will destroy your marriage, your church, our nation, and your soul.

The message of this feast? Redemption is to be followed by a holy life and right living. We may not be immediately punished for disobedience as the Israelites were, but we will pay the price for sin. There is a payday!

Father God, we stand before You as sinful people. No one is blameless, nor could we ever hope to be except through the sanctifying blood of Your Son. Forgive us, Father, when we fail You, and wash us in the cleansing power of Your forgiveness.

Day Two: Unleavened Bread in New Testament Times

*B*y the time of Christ, the Hebrew word *Pesach*, which means "passing by or over," had come to signify the amalgamation of the Feasts of Passover and Unleavened Bread. As time passed, each element of the Passover meal took on a spiritual and symbolic significance. The bread, which had been hastily baked in the exodus from Egypt, became known as *matzah*, and the bitter herbs eaten at the Passover meal, said to represent the bitter lot of the Hebrews in slavery, as *maror*. Even the mix of fruit and nuts, the *charoset*, was imbued with meaning. Of a rough texture, the mixture was said to represent the mortar mixed by the Jews as they labored to build monuments for the Egyptian pharaohs.

Look back with me now to the time of Pesach in the time of Christ. On the fourteenth day of Abib, as the Levites and priests gather in the Temple to begin preparing for the sacrifice of thousands of Passover lambs, Jewish families throughout the Holy City are finishing the annual "housecleaning" ritual they began the day before. The *chamets*, or bread and sour dough, must be entirely swept away, with not a crumb remaining. The woman of the house has scrubbed every dish and cooking utensil or purchased new ones. By the light of oil lamps, the women and children scour the house and empty baskets, literally cleansing the house of every particle of leaven. Once they have finished, the father of the home walks slowly through the house, carefully searching for any forgotten bit of leaven.

Once the bits of leavened bread are collected, everyone in Jerusalem waits for the official signal to burn the chamets. This signal will be given by the priests in the Temple, who use two disqualified loaves as a thanks offering. These two large loaves are placed in plain sight on top of the outside colonnade of the Temple. As long as the two loaves are visible, leavened bread may still be eaten. When one loaf is taken away, the people must stop eating chamets. When the second loaf is removed, it is time to burn any and all pieces of leavened bread.[1]

> *C*hamets symbolizes the "risen yeast" in man, the egoism, arrogance, and self-centeredness which separate him from God. The mystics compared chamets to a dark cloud of egoism which blots out the divine light, and they likened eating it on Passover to worshipping idols.
> —RABBI ALAN UNTERMAN

Obviously, this system of signals won't be visible to every family in Jerusalem. A backup signal is therefore arranged, and two cows are set to plowing the earth on top of the Mount of Olives. As long as both cows are yoked to the plow, chamets may still be eaten. The unhitching of the first cow is a signal to cease eating leavened bread, and the removal of the second is the signal to burn the chamets.

It is interesting, isn't it, that the chamets, representing sin, are obliterated by fire? Time and time again in the Bible we see that fire, both literal and metaphorical, is a purifying force. Sodom and Gomorrah were destroyed by fire; many sacrifices

were hallowed by flames. Paul writes that one day every Christian's deeds will be tested in the same way:

> Each one's work will become clear; for the Day will declare it, because it will be revealed by fire; and the fire will test each one's work, of what sort it is. If anyone's work which he has built on it endures, he will receive a reward. If anyone's work is burned, he will suffer loss; but he himself will be saved, yet so as through fire. (1 Cor. 3:13–15 NKJV)

At the end of the age, the earth itself will be purged by fire: "But the day of the Lord will come as a thief in the night, in which the heavens will pass away with a great noise, and the elements will melt with fervent heat; both the earth and the works that are in it will be burned up" (2 Peter 3:10 NKJV).

The Jews of Jerusalem in A.D. 33 aren't thinking about the end of the age, however. Their hearts and hopes are fixed upon the Messiah. They pour a cup of wine for Elijah and prop the doors of their houses open in the steadfast hope that the prophet might appear. Since the deliverance from Egypt occurred in the month of Nisan (Abib), the Jews believe that the messianic redemption will also occur in Nisan.

Few of them realize that their hopes and prayers have been answered. More than seven dozen messianic prophecies have been fulfilled on this night; yet most are too preoccupied with worries about Roman domination to realize that the greatest victory, a *spiritual* victory, has been won only a short distance outside the city wall . . . on the hill called Golgotha.

Did the Jews of Jesus' day recognize their Messiah in the prophets' words? Did they read the prophecies with understanding and realize that Messiah walked among them? Many of them were blind, but others saw the truth. Some were like

Simeon, the devout Jewish man whom the Spirit of God had promised that he would live to see the Lord's Christ. Moved by the Spirit thirty-three years before this particular Passover, Simeon had ventured into the Temple courts and waited day after day, believing the time was right, knowing that God had spoken to his heart. Perhaps his friends and family mocked him; we don't know.

But one day a young couple walked into the Temple courtyard with a pair of birds for a purification sacrifice, a simple offering from simple people. The woman carried a swaddled infant in her arms, and at the sight of the baby Simeon felt his heart leap within him.

He knew.

She carried the Anointed One. The Messiah.

Walking forward on legs that suddenly felt as insubstantial as air, the old man took the child from the startled young woman. Lifting the child heavenward, he praised God, saying, "Lord, now You are letting Your servant depart in peace, according to Your word; for my eyes have seen Your salvation which You have prepared before the face of all peoples, a light to bring revelation to the Gentiles, and the glory of Your people Israel" (Luke 2:29–32 NKJV).

A prophetess, Anna, stood nearby. Was she shocked to see Simeon lifting a baby when the entire nation expected a warrior Messiah? Was she surprised by his reference to the Gentiles?

No. Drawing near, she gave thanks to God and joined Simeon in telling everyone nearby that the child would bring about the redemption of Jerusalem.

As He did, thirty-three years later, on Calvary's hill. Most Jews were still expecting a soldier-Messiah. They ate their seder that night with one eye turned toward their open doors,

their ears straining for the sounds of deliverance, a Messiah's rallying cry to unite against Rome.

While the Anointed One of God, God's Passover Lamb, quietly lowered His head and surrendered His life. He paid a debt He did not owe; I owed a debt I could not pay.

Heavenly Father, how we thank You that You sent Your Son to be Savior not only to the chosen people, but to the Gentiles. You have poured out Your Spirit on all flesh, and we praise You for Your goodness.

DAY THREE: UNLEAVENED BREAD IN THE PRESENT DAY

he highlight of a contemporary Jewish Pesach observance is the seder. Contemporary Jews consider it a *mitzvah* (a commandment or religious duty) to follow the Old Testament custom and remove leaven from the home prior to the beginning of Pesach. Leaven includes products made from wheat, barley, rye, oats, and spelt (a type of wheat grown in Europe) that have been permitted to rise or ferment.

Many families involve their children in a playful search for leaven. Often the mother will scrupulously clean the home, carefully leaving bits of bread in places where the children are sure to find them. The night before Pesach, with the aid of a flashlight or candles, the children conduct a search and even the tiniest bits of leaven are collected in a bag. The next morning, the leaven is burned with the following blessing: "Blessed are You, O Lord our God, Ruler of the universe, who hallows us with mitzvot and commands us to burn chamets."

During the entire seven days of Pesach, leavened products are not to be used or eaten. By consciously choosing to avoid certain foods, participants in Pesach are constantly reminded of the festival and their identity as Jews.

Hospitality is another commandment of Pesach. The Jewish community strives to make certain no one is excluded from the festive occasion, for no one should have to celebrate Passover alone. Do you remember the many stories Jesus told about the man who prepared a banquet and invited guests to come? Jesus may well have been referring to the seder, for all

are invited to participate in the table that celebrates redemption.

At the seder meal, a plate is set in front of each guest. Upon each plate are arranged three separate pieces of matzah—two to represent the traditional loaves set out in the ancient Temple during Sabbaths and festivals, and a third to symbolize Passover itself. Also on the plate is a roasted shank bone to represent the sacrificial Passover lamb; parsley or green herbs, symbolizing the growth of spring; the top of a horseradish root to symbolize the bitter travail of slavery in Egypt; charoset, representing the mortar of Egypt; and a roasted egg, representing the chagigah, and the triumph of life over death.[2]

On the seder table you will also find a special cup set for Elijah. Because Elijah is supposed to return as a forerunner of

the Messiah, a cup is poured for the prophet in the hope that he will appear, thus speeding the Messiah's appearance. This belief is based on Malachi 4:5–6, in which the prophet relates God's promise: "Behold, I will send you Elijah the prophet before the coming of the great and dreadful day of the LORD. And he will turn the hearts of the fathers to the children, and the hearts of the children to their fathers, lest I come and strike the earth with a curse" (NKJV).

Near the conclusion of the seder, someone will rise and open the door, ostensibly for Elijah, though others have said it is a demonstration that Pesach eve is a "night of watching unto the Lord." The origin of this custom is veiled, but it probably has something to do with the commandment of hospitality.

No seder would be complete without the *Haggadah* (Hebrew for "Passover story"). This book, containing songs and recitations nearly two thousand years old, is the consistent ingredient that makes each seder a living, breathing link to the past and future. It enables each family to tell the story of God's redemption from Egypt as commanded in the Bible.

The *Haggadah* includes a biblical selection about the Exodus, psalms of praise, rabbinic homilies, hymns, and children's songs that are sung at the conclusion of the meal. It also contains instructions about the ritual eating of *matzah* and *maror*, and about the drinking of the traditional four cups of wine.

The four cups of wine symbolize four "I will"s of God's redemption mentioned in Exodus 6:6–7: "Therefore say to the children of Israel: 'I am the LORD; *I will bring you out* from under the burdens of the Egyptians, *I will rescue you* from their bondage, and *I will redeem you* with an outstretched arm and with great judgments. *I will take you as My people*, and I will be

your God. Then you shall know that I am the LORD your God who brings you out from under the burdens of the Egyptians" (NKJV emphasis added). Red wine is used to remember the blood of the Passover lamb, which the Israelites smeared on their doorposts in Egypt.

Among the *Haggadah*'s contents are the four questions that must be asked by the youngest member of the family, the list of the ten plagues (during the chanting of which a drop of wine is spilled for each plague), and the wish to meet "next year in Jerusalem."[3]

Though the wording of the four questions and their responses have changed over the years and some of the folk songs are only four or five hundred years old, parts of the *Haggadah* were recited by Jesus and His family. It is also traditional to sing Psalms 115 through 118 at Passover, for these psalms record the certainty of God's undying love for Israel.

There's an old song, however, that I like to think of at Passover. It reminds me of the Pesach commandment for hospitality, and I can just picture the Savior standing in the doorway of His heavenly home, offering His hospitality to any who would come in and dine with Him:

Ho, everyone who is thirsty in spirit,
Ho, everyone who is weary and sad,
Come to the fountain, there's fullness in Jesus.
All that you're longing for, come and be glad.

Day Four: Unleavened Bread in Prophecy

*T*he overall prophetic picture of the Feast of Unleavened Bread has already been fulfilled, yet its observance contains images of other events yet to come. For an individual with spiritual eyes to see, the entire Passover meal is a picture of the death and resurrection of Christ. In the middle of the ritual, a piece of matzo (which is striped and pierced in the baking process) is broken into three pieces, symbolizing God the Father, Son, and Holy Spirit. The second piece, the *afikomen*, is wrapped in white linen and hidden away for a little while, then found amid great rejoicing.

What an incredible picture and prediction of how Jesus Christ, the Bread of Life, would be wounded with the stripes of a whip, pierced with a spear, wrapped in linen, and hidden away in a borrowed tomb. On the night Jesus was betrayed, He ate the Last Supper (so called because it was the last meal in which leavened bread could be eaten before Passover) with His disciples and told them that the bread was His body that was to be broken for them.

Just as the matzo at the Feast of Unleavened Bread is without leaven, Jesus was without sin. His body was hidden away for three days, but then He rose and reappeared on the earth amid great rejoicing.

An old Jewish tradition held that the group of banqueters could not leave the seder table unless all had tasted of the afikomen. Oh, that all might taste and see that the Lord is good!

Consider also the cup of Elijah, ceremonially poured for

the prophet and left untouched throughout the seder meal. Though many theologians believe Elijah will appear as one of the two witnesses mentioned in Revelation 11:3, Jesus told His disciples that John the Baptist was the forerunner prophesied in Malachi. "And if you are willing to receive it," Jesus said, "he [John the Baptist] is Elijah who is to come" (Matt. 11:14; see also Matt. 17:10–13 NKJV).

One of the most striking prophecies fulfilled at the Passover during which Jesus died comes from the book of Daniel:

> Seventy weeks are determined
> For your people and for your holy city,
> To finish the transgression,
> To make an end of sins,
> To make reconciliation for iniquity,
> To bring in everlasting righteousness,
> To seal up vision and prophecy,
> And to anoint the Most Holy.
> Know therefore and understand,
> That from the going forth of the command
> To restore and build Jerusalem
> Until Messiah the Prince,
> There shall be seven weeks and sixty-two weeks;
> The street shall be built again, and the wall,
> Even in troublesome times.
> And after the sixty-two weeks
> Messiah shall be cut off, but not for Himself;
> And the people of the prince who is to come
> Shall destroy the city and the sanctuary. (Dan. 9:24–26 NKJV)

The "seventy weeks" is generally understood to mean 7

times 70 years, or 490 years. Daniel subdivides the 70 weeks into 7 weeks, 62 weeks, and 1 additional week. Each week represents seven years on man's calendar.

What do the seventy weeks mean? The interpretation never fails to send a holy thrill through my soul.

The decree to rebuild Jerusalem—issued during the time of Nehemiah—was given in 445 B.C. For forty-nine years (Daniel's first period of seven weeks), Nehemiah and his men labored to rebuild the wall, and the work was completed in 396 B.C., even in "troublesome times."

Daniel's second period of time, 62 weeks, represents 434 years. The brilliant scholar and Bible student, Sir Robert Anderson, has calculated that if one begins counting days on March 14, 445 B.C. (the accepted date of the decree to rebuild Jerusalem), and moves forward, Daniel's timeline ends at the

day Jesus made His triumphal entry into Jerusalem![4] And that very night, the chief priests, the scribes, and the leaders of the people began to plot His death. Within days, Israel's Messiah was "cut off," just as Daniel predicted.

But one week remains on Daniel's timeline. As a footnote, Daniel added that the people of the

prince who is to come (the Antichrist of Revelation) shall destroy the city and the sanctuary—just as the Romans destroyed Jerusalem and the Temple in A.D. 70. The Antichrist who is yet to come will arise from a revived Roman Empire, he will confirm a covenant with Israel for one week (seven days equals seven years), but in the middle of the week (after three and one-half years), he will bring an end to sacrifice and offering in the rebuilt Temple. "On a wing of the temple he will set up an abomination that causes desolation, until the end that is decreed is poured out on him" (Dan. 9:27 NIV).

God has called a "time-out," as it were, in Daniel's prophetic seventy weeks. At Calvary God stepped in and stopped the clock, but soon the Lamb of God will blow His trumpet and Daniel's final week will begin.

During His triumphal entry into Jerusalem, Jesus looked over His beloved city and wept, saying:

> If you had known, even you, especially in this your day, the things that make for your peace! But now they are hidden from your eyes. For the days will come upon you when your enemies will build an embankment around you, surround you and close you in on every side, and level you, and your children within you, to the ground; and they will not leave in you one stone upon another, because you did not know the time of your visitation. (Luke 19:42–44 NKJV)

This prophecy was exactly fulfilled to the jot and tittle when the Romans under Titus (A.D. 70) and Hadrian (A.D. 135) surrounded the city in a massive siege and crucified any Jew who tried to escape Jerusalem. There were as many as five

hundred Jews being crucified at one time outside the walls of the city of Jerusalem.

How can we fault the Jews of Jesus' day for not seeing Him when so many people of our day cannot recognize the truth in Daniel's prophecy? The Jews had the word of the prophets to illustrate their future; we have prophecies that illustrate ours just as fully. God never intended for man to understand the future by human wisdom; true wisdom requires faith in the Scripture as the inspired Word of God that reveals our future in complete detail.

Father, help us to realize that we live in the age of grace. The time of judgment is coming, the time of grace will soon end, and those who are lost will find themselves caught up in Daniel's final week and the wrath of Almighty God.

Renew in us a sense of urgency; awaken within us a compassion for lost souls. Revive us again, O Lord our God.

Day Five: Unleavened Bread Made Personal

$\mathscr{B}$efore Pesach begins, every Jew is to remove all traces of leaven, a symbol of sin, from his house. Observant Jews rid their homes of leaven through a cleaning ritual—sweeping, dusting, and searching for any place in which leaven might be hiding.

My friend, too many of us today are unwilling to search our hearts for sin. During the past forty years secular humanism has stripped any sense of absolute right and wrong from American minds. Our children now live by "lifeboat" ethics. With the Ten Commandments thrown out of our classrooms by the Supreme Court and the ACLU seeking freedom *from* religion, our students no longer believe in sin. Liars—in high places—are excused as being "extroverted" or "imaginative." Adultery is called "free love." It's not free and it's not love—it's lust. Love gives a ring and makes a covenant commitment in marriage. Lust gives a condom and sexual diseases.

Four thousand babies are murdered every day in America's abortion mills. Partial-birth abortion, in which a doctor pierces the skull of a baby with scissors and extracts its brains with a suction device, is more common than the experts would have you believe. It is nothing less than cold-blooded murder! The spreading culture of death spews blood and gore into our living rooms as week after week television offers an unending buffet of murder and mayhem.

Why do politicians pound their chests for the TV cameras, lamenting that our school playgrounds resemble a battlefield

covered with the blood of our dead and dying children? If a politician has zero respect for life by condoning partial-birth abortion, why are they surprised when a teenager takes a gun and murders another student? When our national leaders have no respect for life, why are we amazed when our children pick up guns with the intent to kill?

Our political leaders are marching at the front of the parade leading to the moral abyss. The Clinton administration's moral transgressions are too many to list. At the beginning of the 1992 election we were told that "character doesn't count," but it does, my friend, it does!

A lie is a lie!

Truth is the truth!

Sin is still sin and God forgives nothing until there is genuine confession of sin and repentance.

> *M*ankind is still in need of a Savior, for sin is still sin though we call it by many new psychological names.
> —F. M. SWAFFIELD

Our leaders are the mirror image of the American people, and America has lost her moral compass. How can a politician have sky-high approval ratings while admittedly swimming in one major disgrace after another? He can't, unless there is no standard of righteousness, no concept of sin, no notion of honor, no understanding of integrity. Without these things, the country quickly sinks into the darkness of moral blindness. No one is listening to the Bible's warning that "righteousness exalts a nation, but sin is a reproach to any people" (Prov. 14:34 NKJV).

As I write this, weeks after President Clinton's confession of an "inappropriate relationship" with Monica Lewinsky, I am constantly hearing the refrain that "private sin has nothing to do with a person's ability to perform his public responsibilities." Wrong! Private sin affects everything a man or woman touches, because it reveals true *character*, and character is the basis of every relationship.

Yes, the president asked for forgiveness and it should be extended to him by all people of faith. But there is a dramatic difference between forgiveness and trust. Trust is the glue that holds a democracy or a marriage together. Lying destroys trust and requires the passing of time before trust can be restored.

In God's mind, private sin certainly does affect other people! When Achan stole the Babylonian garment, gold, and silver from defeated Jericho, God commanded that he be stoned to death with his wife and children in order to put sin out of Israel. Achan's "private sin" destroyed his entire family.

The president's sin has wounded his family, it has destroyed Monica Lewinsky, and scarred Paula Jones, Gennifer Flowers, and Kathleen Willey. His sin has mocked the dignity of the Oval Office and made our government a laughingstock throughout the world.

There's a Jewish story that beautifully illustrates this principle: A group of people were traveling in a ship, when one of the passengers took a drill and began to bore a hole under his seat. "What are you doing?" the others protested.

"What has this to do with you?" the man answered. "I am boring the hole under my own seat, not yours."

"It has everything to do with us," they answered. "Because the water will come in and drown us all."[5]

What's gone wrong in America? We can't cast the blame

solely at the feet of politicians, for the church is certainly part of the problem. The "greasy grace" preached from pulpits across this land set the stage for our brain-dead morality. People wink at sin and transgress with smiles on their faces. The self-satisfied settle back and smugly salve their consciences with a quick quip: "I'm covered by grace."

Hear me! Greasy grace only forgives the sin. God's grace forgives the *sinner*. If you want to be truly forgiven, go to God, not to those who will tell you that "slipping up" is only natural and to be expected. Quit trying to analyze your sin and just confess your sin.

Let me remind you of the eternal facts: Grace was never intended to be a license to sin. Extending forgiveness to anyone without demanding change in their conduct makes the grace of God an accomplice to evil. To the woman caught in adultery, Jesus said, "Go and sin no more." He expected her to change. He still expects transformation. Friends, pay attention to the Feast of Unleavened Bread. God has zero tolerance for sin.

God would have spared Sodom and Gomorrah if He could have found just ten righteous people within those walls. But because of the total moral collapse, He annihilated that entire society. Do you think God is going to make an exception for America? The eyes of God are studying our society at this very moment. If the day comes when He can't find enough people to retard our country's moral and spiritual rot, God will crush this nation as well.

Do you want God's blessing upon your life? Then hunger and thirst for righteousness! Jesus said, "But seek first the kingdom of God and His righteousness, and all these things shall be added to you" (Matt. 6:33 NKJV).

Do you want God's protection? Live a righteous and pure

life! "The eyes of the LORD are on the righteous," wrote the psalmist, "and His ears are open to their cry" (Ps. 34:15 NKJV).

Do you want God to provide for your children? Live a godly life! In Psalm 37:25, the psalmist assures us, "I have been young, and now am old; Yet I have not seen the righteous forsaken, Nor his descendants begging bread" (NKJV).

Do you want God to answer your prayers? Live righteously! "The LORD is far from the wicked," Solomon wrote, "but He hears the prayer of the righteous" (Prov. 15:29 NKJV). James assures us that the prayer of a righteous man avails much (5:16), and the psalmist adds a warning: "If I regard iniquity [sin] in my heart, The Lord will not hear" (Ps. 66:18 NKJV).

Dear friend, America's best national defense policy does not lie in producing more stealth bombers, manufacturing more condoms, propounding more sex education, or providing more clean needles for drug addicts. Our only hope lies in a revival of the righteousness of God to sweep this nation. America will either have a revival of righteousness or rebellion in the streets.

Father God, help me to be aware of the sins in my life. Remind me that as a Christian I represent Christ on earth, and my name is intimately wrapped up in Jesus' reputation.

The Feast of Firstfruits

APRIL 1-7
1999

APRIL 20-26
2000

APRIL 8-14
2001

MARCH 28 -
APRIL 3
2002

APRIL 17-23
2003

APRIL 6-12
2004

APRIL 24-30
2005

Day One: The Feast of Firstfruits

When God instructed Moses to tell the children of Israel about the Feast of Firstfruits, the entire festival must have seemed like a fantasy. While they were still wandering in the desert, Moses told the people they would enter a land flowing with milk and honey. He foretold that they would plant crops, reap bountiful harvests, and travel to a place of the Lord's choosing to offer the firstfruits of their harvest to God.

The ex-slaves who listened to Moses were refugees, and when he spoke they stood in the midst of a rocky wilderness. The very idea of a bountiful harvest in a fertile land was foreign to them. In Egypt, if they planted crops at all, the harvest of that crop belonged to Pharaoh. *Everything* belonged to Pharaoh, even their lives.

But God had brought them out, set them free, and promised that He would lead them into a land fertile beyond their wildest imagining. Surely Moses' depiction of the promised land sounded like heaven!

> And the LORD spoke to Moses, saying, "Speak to the children of Israel, and say to them: 'When you come into the land which I give to you, and reap its harvest, then you shall bring a sheaf of the firstfruits of your harvest to the priest. He shall wave the sheaf before the LORD, to be accepted on your behalf; on the day after the Sabbath the priest shall wave it.

"And you shall offer on that day, when you wave the sheaf, a male lamb of the first year, without blemish, as a burnt offering to the LORD. Its grain offering shall be two-tenths of an ephah of fine flour mixed with oil, an offering made by fire to the LORD, for a sweet aroma; and its drink offering shall be of wine, one-fourth of a hin [one quart].

"You shall eat neither bread nor parched grain nor fresh grain until the same day that you have brought an offering to your God; it shall be a statute forever throughout your generations in all your dwellings." (Lev. 23:9–14 NKJV)

The Feast of Firstfruits commemorates resurrection, for God lifted an enslaved, spiritually dead people and blessed them with new life. In Egypt the Israelites had all but forgotten God; Moses had to forcefully remind them that their forefathers had served the unseen and all-knowing God of Abraham, Isaac, and Jacob. Furthermore, Moses told them, this mighty God had heard their cries of misery. He had remembered His covenant with Israel, and He was going to bring them out of bondage and into a land flowing with milk and honey.

The Israelites joyfully packed camels and donkeys for the trip out of Egypt; they left *Mizraim* (the fortified land) with light hearts and hopeful spirits, content to know that they had but to follow Moses and they would be free of Egypt's tyranny.

But then they came to the Red Sea . . . and their dreams withered in the heat of the desert sun.

How were they supposed to cross the sea? God hadn't said anything about taking boats. Worse yet, there was no time to build rafts, for already they could see a line of

advancing chariots on the horizon. Pharaoh, with his entire army, was rapidly approaching.

As one, the people lifted their voices against their leader. "Were there no graves in Egypt, so you led us out here to die in the wilderness? Why have you done this to us? In Egypt, didn't we tell you to leave us alone? It would have been better for us to serve the Egyptians than to die out here in the wilderness or drown in the Red Sea."

Moses, who had learned long before that nothing was impossible for God, answered with an authoritative voice: "Do not be afraid. Stand still, and see the salvation of the Lord. For the Egyptians, whom you see today, you will see again no more forever. The Lord will fight for you, and you shall hold your peace."

Then the Lord, who was probably growing a little impatient with the wavering people He had just rescued, asked Moses, "Why are you crying to Me? Tell the children of Israel to go forward. Lift up your rod, and stretch out your hand over the sea and divide it. And the children of Israel shall go on dry ground through the midst of the sea."

Then Moses stretched out his hand, and the Lord caused the water to go back by a strong east wind. He turned that soggy seabed into dry land, and the waters divided into two walls: one on the right hand and another on the left. (See Ex. 14.)

I wish I'd been there. I've seen Hollywood versions of the miracle, of course, but those filmmakers haven't even come close to depicting the miracle God provided for His people.

On that day, the children of Israel walked into the depths of the Red Sea and came out the other side alive. They marched into a watery grave and God raised them on the other bank a nation of free people.

On a practical level, the offering of firstfruits was a sign of what God had done—brought forth the ripening of the grain—and what God was *going* to do—complete a bountiful harvest for His people. On a spiritual level, the offering of firstfruits was meant to remind the people of how God had delivered them and illustrate how He was going to deliver them through His Son.

When the Israelites went down into the depths of the Red Sea and came up alive on the other side, they were demonstrating how God would bring salvation to the entire world. Consider the parallels: At the Red Sea, the Israelites walked down through the waters and were raised to walk as free and victorious people! In baptism, we are lowered under the water to represent our identification with Christ's death and raised to walk in newness of life. God fought the battle for the children of Israel just as Christ defeated death for us.

Hallelujah!

I will sing to the LORD,
For He has triumphed gloriously!
The horse and its rider
He has thrown into the sea!
The LORD is my strength and song,
And He has become my salvation.
—Exodus 15:1–2, 6 NKJV

Amen!

Day Two: Firstfruits in the Time of Christt

*T*he term *firstfruits* refers to the first portion of the harvest, a portion specially dedicated to God. The firstfruits were a pledge of the greater harvest to follow, and the offering of them was a way of expressing trust in God's provision. Just as He provided the firstfruits, so He would also provide the rest of the crops the people needed.[1]

By New Testament times, the Feast of Firstfruits as explained in Leviticus 23 had been swallowed up in the rites of Passover. According to Leviticus 23:11, the observance of firstfruits was supposed to occur on the day after the Sabbath in Passover week ("on the day after the Sabbath the priest shall wave it" [NKJV]).

The Sadducees, the party of conservative priests, interpreted this to mean that the *omer*, or sheaf of grain, should be offered the first Sunday of Pesach. The Pharisees, however, who sought to interpret the Torah according to contemporary practice, interpreted the word *Sabbath* to mean "day of rest," not "Saturday." According to the Pharisees, it was necessary to offer the omer on the sixteenth day of Nisan. Orthodox Judaism has adopted the Pharisees' approach, and today the Feast of Firstfruits is considered to fall on the sixteenth day of Nisan, with Pentecost falling fifty days later.[2]

During Old Testament times, especially during the spiritual "dark ages" of the divided kingdom, the Jews observed Passover and the Feast of Unleavened Bread in their homes, not at the Temple. They followed these two rites with the cer-

emony of the omer, in which the first sheaf of newly cut barley was offered to the priest at the nearest altar.

By the time of Christ, people routinely traveled to Jerusalem to offer their Passover sacrifices in the Temple. On the Sunday after Passover, they journeyed to the Temple again to offer a symbolic sheaf of barley cut from the newly budding harvest.

The society of Jesus' day revolved around agriculture, and Jesus often spoke in metaphors about crops and fields and harvests. During His final Passover week, a short while after the triumphal entry, the Lord called His disciples near and told them, "The hour has come that the Son of Man should be glorified. Most assuredly, I say to you, unless a grain of wheat falls into the ground and dies, it remains alone; but if it dies, it produces much grain" (John 12:23–24 NKJV).

The disciples were confused and bothered by Jesus' words. They still had not grasped the truth that Jesus had come to die. They wanted Him to be the Messiah, but they wanted Him to raise an army and overthrow their Roman oppressors. They did not want Him to die . . . and they most assuredly did not want to die with Him.

Jesus tried to explain that He would be lifted up in order to draw all men to Himself. He had not come to be the reigning Messiah, but the Lamb of God. He had not come to rule, but to die as a sacrifice for all . . . to fall and die, like a grain of wheat, in order to be resurrected and bring forth new life.

Jesus understood that He would die on Passover, His body would lie in the tomb during the Feast of Unleavened Bread, and He would rise on the Feast of Firstfruits, the first of many to come. He would be the first to defeat death eternally, but an entire harvest of victorious souls would follow.

Paul explained it in 1 Corinthians 15:20–23:

> But now Christ is risen from the dead, and has become the firstfruits of those who have fallen asleep. For since by man came death, by Man also came the resurrection of the dead. For as in Adam all die, even so in Christ all shall be made alive. But each one in his own order: Christ the first-fruits, afterward those who are Christ's at His coming. (NKJV)

Oh, there were many Jews who wanted to follow Jesus when He fed five thousand with five biscuits and two little fish! There were others who would have gladly pledged their lives when He raised Lazarus from the dead. They saw Him as a military leader who could feed thousands and resurrect wounded warriors—His army would surely be invincible against the Romans!

But Jesus had come to earth for entirely different reasons—reasons they could not understand.

The multiplied thousands who followed Jesus did not surrender the idea that He would be their reigning Messiah until they saw Him hanging from a Roman cross. Even after His resurrection and His repeated denials that He would not be the Messiah they expected, His disciples were still clinging to the last thread of hope that He would smash Rome. "Lord," they asked Him, "will You at this time restore the kingdom to Israel?" (Acts 1:6 NKJV).

Except a grain of wheat falls into the ground and dies . . .

I can almost see the Savior shaking His head in regret at their dull-wittedness. They were so slow to understand! On the cross, He defeated a far greater foe than Rome. He won the right to offer us more than earthly position or power.

Just as Israel marched out of the Red Sea to stand on solid ground, Jesus Christ arose the Victor over death, hell, and the grave. Just as Jesus predicted, He arose the mighty Conqueror over powers and principalities. Rome could not convict Him, the Cross could not conquer Him, and the grave could not contain Him! Like a grain of wheat, He arose on the day of the Feast of Firstfruits to bring life to millions!

Father God, I thank You that Jesus is alive this very moment, sitting at Your right hand, awaiting the hour of His second coming when kings, queens, presidents, and prime ministers shall bow at His feet and confess that He is Lord!

Day Three: Present-Day Feast of Firstfruits

s we've already learned, Leviticus 23:15 states that the counting of the fifty-day period from Passover until Pentecost begins on the day after the Sabbath. According to the Talmud, the Sadducees took the word Sabbath literally and began to count the day after the Sabbath, which occurred during the festival of Pesach. Thus the Feast of Firstfruits always fell on Sunday and the date of Pentecost varied from year to year. However, since the Pharisees understood Sabbath to mean the first day of Pesach, they began counting on the day after the Feast of Unleavened Bread, the sixteenth day of Nisan, thus establishing a fixed date for Pentecost.[3]

In the Zola Levitt Ministries July 1995 newsletter, Thomas S. McCall raises an interesting point about why the date may have been changed:

> We have no proof, but suggest that the change came some time after the resurrection of Christ and before the destruction of the Temple. Think of the impact Jewish believers must have had as they described the Lord's resurrection on the Sunday of Passover week at Firstfruits and the coming of the Spirit seven Sundays later on Pentecost. The leaders must have been hard pressed to explain away the relevance of the feasts and their fulfillment in the Messiah. The solution they came up with was to obfuscate the calendar in such a way as to make the connection less clear between the feasts and their fulfillment in Christ and the

Holy Spirit. The strategy apparently worked because most Jewish people today see no connection whatever between the feasts and the Messiah. By the time Josephus wrote his history about the fall of Jerusalem in 70 AD, the Jewish authorities had established the concept that Firstfruits was always on Nisan 16, and Pentecost on Sivan six.[4]

Jesus Christ, the Lamb of God, died on Passover and rose to new life on Sunday, the Feast of Firstfruits! Can't you see the glorious connection? Though the Pharisees changed the date, if we celebrate the Feast of Firstfruits on Sunday as God commanded, we see a clear picture of Christ's resurrection! Christ rose as the first to be resurrected, but all who believe in Him shall likewise rise from the dead at the Rapture, the final "harvest."

Overshadowed as it is by Pesach, the Feast of Firstfruits has all but vanished from the modern Jewish calendar. Wave offerings have not been practiced since the destruction of the Temple in A.D. 70, and many of the rites and rituals associated with the Feast of Firstfruits have been transferred to the Feast of Pentecost, also known as Shavuot. But though the Jews no longer observe the Feast of Firstfruits as described in Leviticus 23, there is no denying the link between Passover and Pentecost. The fifty-day period between Pesach and Pentecost is known as *Sefirah* (counting) or *Sefirat Ha-omer* (counting the wave offering).

The Jews count the days until Pentecost, or Shavuot, and wait for the next festival . . . just as they wait for the Messiah.

Ah, my Christian friend, if you're feeling a little smug, deny that feeling! If we have received more light than many of the Jewish people, it is because of God's grace and mercy, not because we merit any special favors. God still loves the children

of Abraham, they still are His chosen people. (See Romans 11:1, 11, and 18.)

Back in the wilderness, Israel willingly followed God, believing His promise to bring them to a land flowing with milk and honey. "Israel was to be a pledge of a greater harvest inasmuch as she would experience God's redemption and witness of this redemption to the nations," says Rich Robinson of Jews for Jesus, "that they, too, might come to know the God of Israel."[5]

When will Israel welcome the Messiah and experience its harvest? Look at Romans 11:25: "For I do not desire, brethren," Paul writes, "that you should be ignorant of this mystery, lest you should be wise in your own opinion, that blindness in part has happened to Israel until the fullness of the Gentiles has come in" (NKJV). The word translated *fullness* is the Greek word *pleroma*. The word refers not to a numerical capacity, but to a sense of completeness.

"The completion of the mission to the Gentiles will result in, or lead to, Israel's 'fullness' or 'completion' (Rom. 11:12), her 'acceptance' (Rom. 11:15)," write scholars Walter C. Kaiser Jr., Peter H. Davids, F. F. Bruce, and Manfred T. Brauch in *Hard Sayings of the Bible*.

> Paul proclaims this future realization of God's intention as "a mystery" (Rom. 11:25) . . . The most instructive parallel to this text—which envisions the grafting of both Gentile and Jew into the same olive tree—is Ephesians 3:3–6, where Paul says that the content of the "mystery of Christ" is the inclusion of the Gentiles as fellow heirs of the promise with Jews in the new community of Christ's body.[6]

Bible scholars agree that Paul's statement that "all Israel

will be saved" means Israel "as a whole," not every single individual. Just as the phrase "the fullness of the Gentiles" (Rom. 11:25 NKJV) does not mean every single Gentile will accept Jesus as Messiah. But when the "fullness of the Gentiles" has come, that is, when the Gentiles' time of grace is completed, then God will remove Israel's blindness (Rom. 11:10) to the identity of Messiah and "all Israel will be saved" (Rom. 11:26 NKJV).

Jewish tradition does, interestingly enough, provide one other glorious picture of firstfruits. If you'll recall the creation story in the first chapter of Genesis, God created man on the sixth day and rested on the seventh. On the first day of the week, He created a new world out of chaos and rejoiced that it was good.

Jesus died for mankind on Friday, the sixth day. He rested on the seventh, and rose on Sunday, the first day of the week, bringing new life to all who would accept His redemption from the chaos of sin.

Hallelujah for the Cross!

Father God, we praise You for Your sense of order and completeness. Forgive us for our lack of compassion toward Your chosen people, and forgive us for losing sight of the Jewishness of our Hebrew Savior. We are thankful that the One who hears us is a Rabbi named Jesus of Nazareth.

Day Four: The Prophecy of Firstfruits

The Feast of Firstfruits is a foreshadowing of the work of both Good Friday and Easter. It represents the death and resurrection of Jesus Christ, and when Moses explained the laws concerning the feast, his words painted a picture of what would happen at Calvary.

After dying on Passover, the fourteenth of Nisan, Jesus explored the chambers of death. He vanquished death, hell, and the grave. He arose on Sunday morning, the day of the Feast of Firstfruits, and announced, "I am the resurrection and the life. He who believes in Me, though he may die, he shall live. And whoever lives and believes in Me shall never die" (John 11:25–26 NKJV).

There is no spiritual death for the believer. Though his body may die, his spirit lives on with Christ. And at the Rapture, when Jesus returns to gather His church, the believer who has known physical death will receive a new and perfected, supernatural body.

> But I do not want you to be ignorant, brethren, concerning those who have fallen asleep, lest you sorrow as others who have no hope. For if we believe that Jesus died and rose again, even so God will bring with Him those who sleep in Jesus. For this we say to you by the word of the Lord, that we who are alive and remain until the coming of the Lord will by no means precede those who are asleep. For the Lord Himself will descend from heaven with a shout, with the

voice of an archangel, and with the trumpet of God. And the dead in Christ will rise first. Then we who are alive and remain shall be caught up together with them in the clouds to meet the Lord in the air. And thus we shall always be with the Lord. Therefore comfort one another with these words. (1 Thess. 4:13–18 NKJV)

The Feast of Firstfruits foreshadowed the death and burial of Jesus Christ, but it also foreshadows the resurrection of every believer! We were born in the image of Adam, with finite, fallible bodies. The life we know on earth is not limitless; every moment that passes is one debited from our account. God has numbered our days, for we now live and breathe in Adam's image, the image of a mortal man.

But if we die before the Lord's return, we shall be resurrected

with new bodies! According to the apostle Paul, my resurrection body will be like the glorious resurrected body of Jesus, "who will transform our lowly body that it may be conformed to His glorious body, according to the working by which He is able even to subdue all things to Himself" (Phil. 3:21 NKJV).

I do not know exactly how my supernatural body will be formed, but I know that it will be recognizable. The Bible says that in eternity I shall "know just as I also am known" (1 Cor. 13:12 NKJV). Jesus walked the earth in a supernatural, glorified body after His resurrection, and the disciples recognized Him.

After Jesus rose on the Feast of Firstfruits in a glorified body, He attended several dinners, so I know we can eat with our resurrection bodies. Yes! His body was flesh and bone, so real that He invited His disciples to touch His wounded hands and feet (Luke 24:39–40). Miraculously, however, the Lord's supernatural body was not subject to the earthly laws of gravity and time. On at least two occasions, Jesus demonstrated this truth by walking through a wall and vanishing before the disciples' eyes! (John 20:19; Luke 24:31, 36).

Our resurrection bodies, like the Lord's, will not be subject to aging, disease, or weariness. Speaking of our bodies, Paul writes, "For we know that if our earthly house, this tent, is destroyed, we have a building from God, a house not made with hands, eternal in the heavens" (2 Cor. 5:1 NKJV).

I've saved the best fact for last: Our resurrection bodies will not be influenced by the old fleshly nature. The force that drives us to sin will be dead and permanently buried. The human frailties that even Jesus acknowledged ("the spirit indeed is willing, but the flesh is weak" [Matt. 26:41 NKJV]) will not exist in our supernatural, heavenly bodies.

God not only promised that we would be resurrected, but as Christians we will one day know an indescribable fullness

of the Spirit. In Romans 8:23, Paul wrote that we now have "the firstfruits of the Spirit." Scholar Leon Morris believes that Paul meant "either that the measure of the Holy Spirit that we now have is but a foretaste of the greater measure there will be in the age to come, or that the gift of the Spirit now is a foretaste of the many other blessings we will have in due course."[7]

How did the hymn writer put it? "Blessed assurance, Jesus is mine! O what a foretaste of glory divine!"

A firstfruit is a foretaste of things to come—and the firstfruits of the Spirit that we now enjoy are love, joy, peace, longsuffering, kindness, goodness, faithfulness, gentleness, and self-control (Gal. 5:22–23). If these are but a taste of the glories we shall know in heaven, the human mind cannot conceive all the wonders heaven holds for us!

I praise You, Lord, that one day this body will no longer be troubled with weakness, exhaustion, or sickness. You will wipe the tears from my eyes, and then I will cry no more.

Day Five: Firstfruits Made Personal

*M*ankind has a penchant for celebrating "famous firsts." We all remember that Neil Armstrong was the first man to walk on the moon, but can you remember the name of the second man to step onto the lunar surface? I can't.

The first men to fly? Orville and Wilbur Wright.

The first man to invent American's favorite lunch? The Fourth Earl of Sandwich, in 1762.

The first machine gun? Richard Jordan Gatling, of course.

The first man to raise Himself from the dead? Jesus Christ, on the Feast of Firstfruits.

The apostle James wrote, "Of His own will He brought us forth by the word of truth, that we might be a kind of firstfruits of His creatures" (1:18 NKJV).

The Jews to whom James wrote understood all that James implied when he chose to use the word *firstfruits*. Jesus was like the sheaf of barley waved before the priest, a sign that the harvest had begun and a plentiful crop would soon follow. We are the crop that will follow Jesus, the harvest that will soon go with Him into heaven.

We are also a picture of firstfruits to the world. We do not have our supernatural, resurrection bodies, yet we are a foretaste of what is to come. We have the gifts of the Spirit, and we are a picture of Redeemed Man or Woman. Though we are but a thin shadow of all we will be in eternity, we must still take our calling seriously.

To the church at Ephesus Paul wrote, "I therefore, the pris-

oner of the Lord, beseech you to walk worthy of the calling with which you were called, with all lowliness and gentleness, with longsuffering, bearing with one another in love, endeavoring to keep the unity of the Spirit in the bond of peace. There is one body and one Spirit, just as you were called in one hope of your calling; one Lord, one faith, one baptism; one God and Father of all, who is above all, and through all, and in you all" (Eph. 4:1–6 NKJV).

We are called, my friend, to walk in love, in peace, and in unity. We are called to walk as blameless examples of the firstfruits of the resurrection. Our lives on earth are but a foretaste of eternity to come, but we are all of heaven some people will ever see. Whether we live 70 years or 120, we are to honor God through all of our days. If we come to the end of our lifetime before the Lord returns, we can face death in peace and comfort, knowing that the resurrection is coming.

> I do believe, that die I must,
> And be returned from out my dust:
> I do believe, that when I rise,
> Christ I shall see, with these same eyes.
> —ROBERT HERRICK

Just as the Feast of Firstfruits pictures the death and burial of Jesus Christ, it also assures us of the resurrection of every believer! Our finite, fallible bodies were never intended to last for an eternity, but God will give us incorruptible bodies when the great rapture resurrection takes place.

I am looking forward to the day when I receive my supernatural, glorified, heavenly body, but I am not ready to wish away my remaining days on earth. They, too, are precious.

The psalmist wrote, "Teach us to number our days, That we may gain a heart of wisdom" (Ps. 90:12 NKJV). Oh, that we might realize the truth of those words! You and I have been granted a specific number of days in which to live and accomplish the tasks to which God has called us, and the laws of science have determined that our strength and energy dissipate with every passing year. You may not want to face the fact that we die a little each day, but the truth is inescapable.

In the popular movie *Groundhog Day,* the main character, Phil Connors, was given an infinite number of opportunities to relive a single day until he finally "got it right." The movie was a fantasy, but the lesson Connors learned was a valid one—living for others brings fulfillment, love, and joy.

There's a little verse that was popular years ago, and it has stuck in my memory: "Only one life, and 'twill soon be past. Only what's done for Christ will last."

Take some time today to consider your example as one of the firstfruits of Christ. Are you walking in His will? Are you taking time to read His Word? Is your life a channel through which He blesses others? Will others see Christ in you today?

The days are growing shorter; the time of Christ's appearing is closer today than it was yesterday. But still we are called to walk worthy of His calling. Still we are entrusted with the responsibility of showing the world a foretaste of heaven.

If you grew up singing the old hymns, you'll certainly recall this one by Knowles Shaw. It's a harvest song, and I can't sing it without picturing myself standing before the altar of God, lifting a golden sheaf that represents a lost soul redeemed by Christ.

Sowing in the morning, sowing seeds of kindness,
Sowing in the noontide and the dewy eve;
Waiting for the harvest and the time of reaping,
We shall come rejoicing, bringing in the sheaves.[8]

The Feast
of
Pentecost

MAY 21
1999

JUNE 9
2000

MAY 28
2001

MAY 17
2002

JUNE 6
2003

MAY 26
2004

JUNE 13
2005

Day One: The Feast of Pentecost

*E*xactly fifty days after the Feast of Firstfruits, the celebration and thanksgiving for the completed grain harvest take place. Though this feast is similar to the Festival of Firstfruits, the Feast of Pentecost, or *Shavuot* (Hebrew for "weeks"), occurs near the end of the harvest instead of at the beginning. Therefore children of Israel were to offer baked loaves of bread instead of raw grain.

God instituted the Feast of Pentecost in order to remind the people that every good and perfect gift comes from Him. When the children of Israel brought in those first crops after reaching the promised land, there was great rejoicing as they celebrated the end of the harvest.

> And you shall count for yourselves from the day after the Sabbath, from the day that you brought the sheaf of the wave offering: seven Sabbaths shall be completed. Count fifty days to the day after the seventh Sabbath; then you shall offer a new grain offering to the LORD. You shall bring from your dwellings two wave loaves of two-tenths of an ephah. They shall be of fine flour; they shall be baked with leaven. They are the firstfruits to the LORD. And you shall offer with the bread seven lambs of the first year, without blemish, one young bull, and two rams. They shall be as a burnt offering to the LORD, with their grain offering and their drink offerings, an offering made by fire for a sweet aroma to the LORD. Then you shall sacrifice one kid of the

goats as a sin offering, and two male lambs of the first year as a sacrifice of a peace offering. The priest shall wave them with the bread of the firstfruits as a wave offering before the LORD, with the two lambs. They shall be holy to the LORD for the priest. And you shall proclaim on the same day that it is a holy convocation to you. You shall do no customary work on it. It shall be a statute forever in all your dwellings throughout your generations. When you reap the harvest of your land, you shall not wholly reap the corners of your field when you reap, nor shall you gather any gleaning from your harvest. You shall leave them for the poor and for the stranger: I am the LORD your God. (Lev. 23:15–22 NKJV)

The instructions concerning the Feast of Pentecost were given years before the Israelites actually celebrated their first harvest in the promised land. Following the Hebrews' miraculous escape from the Red Sea, the children of Israel traveled forty-seven days until they reached the foothills of Mount Sinai. There God instructed Moses to have the people purify themselves. For three days they cleansed themselves and their clothing, for they were a sinful people about to meet with a holy God.

When Moses told the people of the Lord's desire to meet with them, they replied, "All that the LORD has spoken we will do" (Ex. 19:8 NKJV). In Hebrew their reply was *"Na'aseh V'Nishmah,"* which means, *"We agree to do even before we have listened."* Fifty days after crossing the Red Sea, the Israelites fearfully and faithfully approached Mount Sinai, the great mountain of God, to receive the Ten Commandments.

As Moses went up to speak with God, the ground shook and a mighty rushing wind roared over the desert plain. Fire glowed on the mountaintop. According to the Midrash, a

rabbinical commentary on the Scriptures, when God gave the Torah He displayed untold marvels to Israel with His voice. God spoke and the voice reverberated throughout the whole world, and all the people witnessed the thunderings (Ex. 20:18). According to Jewish tradition, when God spoke to Moses, He not only spoke in Hebrew, but His voice split into seventy voices, in seventy languages, so that all the nations should understand . . .[1]

Why seventy languages? In Deuteronomy 32:8–9, the Bible tells us that when the Most High "separated the sons of Adam [at Babel—see Gen. 11:8], He set the boundaries of the [world's] peoples according to the number of the children of Israel." Exodus 1:1–5 gives the number of the children of Israel who went into Egypt at Joseph's invitation as seventy, hence the reasoning of the rabbis who believe God spoke in seventy tongues.

At the time of Pentecost, atop Mount Sinai, God set the stage for the future. As He directed the participants in His Pentecost drama, God wrote prophecy into the plot and demonstrated how He planned to reach the entire Gentile world. The Israelites didn't know it, but as they heard the sound of the trumpet and watched the fire of God descend upon Sinai amid the rushing of a powerful wind, they were seeing what God was going to do fifty days after the resurrection of Jesus Christ!

But the children of Israel didn't realize the full significance of the Mount Sinai experience. They couldn't understand the picture of the two leavened loaves that were to be offered to the Lord at Pentecost—one to represent Israel, one to represent the church, both chosen by God and holy unto Him though sin, or leaven, still exists in them.

But the children of Israel did understand that God had

commanded the people to rejoice and practice generosity during the time of Pentecost. All the people were to rest from their occupational labor on that day, and each man was to treat his neighbor with kindness and compassion. As a reminder, God commanded that the crops should not be completely harvested—the wheat in the corners of the fields was to be left unmolested, and any wheat that fell to the ground was to remain where it was. Strangers in the land and the poor could then glean the field and pick up the remaining grain, thus fending off starvation.

You will no doubt recall the story of the young widow Ruth, a Moabite woman who forsook her Gentile heritage in order to cling to her mother-in-law, Naomi, and follow the God of Israel. Ruth told her mother-in-law, "Entreat me not to leave you, Or to turn back from following after you; For wherever you go, I will go; And wherever you lodge, I will lodge; Your people shall be my people, And your God, my God" (Ruth 1:16 NKJV).

After the death of her husband, Ruth, a Gentile, journeyed with her mother-in-law to the city of Bethlehem in Israel. They arrived at the time of the wheat harvest, but the women had no fields to reap. With no man to provide for either Ruth or Naomi, Ruth began to glean in the wheat field of Boaz, a kinsman of Naomi's. Boaz, in turn, began to love, protect, and provide for Ruth, eventually marrying her and giving her a son. That son, Obed, occupies a privileged position in the lineage of King David and Christ Himself. Ruth was the great-grandmother of King David, perhaps the greatest earthly king Israel has ever known!

The lesson of Ruth is significant in the days of Pentecost, for in its pages the Jews are reminded of God's command to be generous to the stranger (Prov. 21:13). The book of Ruth

also illustrates that Gentiles who accept the God of Israel are welcomed by Him.

I find it interesting that Ruth's story also portrays the work of Christ as redeemer. The concept of the kinsman-redeemer or *goel* (Hebrew for "close relative") is an important picture of the work of Christ. Jesus Christ redeemed us, sinners without hope, just as Boaz redeemed Ruth from poverty and want.

According to Scripture, in order for a kinsman to redeem a soul in need, he must meet three conditions. The *goel* must be able to pay the price of redemption (Ruth 2:1; 1 Peter 1:18, 19); he must be willing to redeem (Ruth 3:11; Matt. 20:28; John 10:15, 18; Heb. 10:7); and he must be free himself—just as Christ was free from the curse of sin.

The Hebrew word *goel*, used thirteen times in the short book of Ruth, presents a clear picture of the mediating work of Christ. In order to redeem Ruth, Boaz bought back the land that had belonged to Naomi's family, took an impoverished Gentile woman as his bride, and lovingly elevated her to a position of prominence.

In the same way, Jesus Christ willingly gave His life as the price of our redemption. He redeemed us from the debt of sin with joy and adopted us as heirs and joint-heirs in the kingdom of God. According to Paul, Gentiles were "aliens from the commonwealth of Israel and strangers from the covenants of promise, having no hope and without God in the world. But now in Christ Jesus you who once were far off have been made near by the blood of Christ" (Eph. 2:12–13 NKJV).

Just as Ruth, a Gentile woman in a Jewish world, had no hope of a future in her mother-in-law, Naomi, so we Gentiles had no hope until we were redeemed by Christ's blood and

grafted into the olive tree (Rom. 11:24) to become partakers of the blessings of Abraham (Gen. 12:1–3).

Heavenly Father, how I praise You that we have redemption through Your blood, the forgiveness of sins, and the riches of Your grace. Like Boaz, who looked upon Ruth, You saw us when we were lost, afraid, and hungry. Your heart was stirred with compassion, and You lifted us up. Thank You, Lord, for considering us. Help us to be aware of the others around us who are lost and afraid.

Day Two: Pentecost in the Time of Christ

*Y*ears after God brought the children of Israel to the Promised Land, the prophet Jeremiah recorded a wonderful prophecy. One day, God promised, mankind would be able to obey Him because of a miracle He would create in the hearts of individuals. The Law would not be engraved in stone or on paper, but on the innermost heart of man:

> Behold, the days are coming, says the LORD, when I will make a new covenant with the house of Israel and with the house of Judah—not according to the covenant that I made with their fathers in the day that I took them by the hand to lead them out of the land of Egypt, My covenant which they broke, though I was a husband to them, says the LORD. But this is the covenant that I will make with the house of Israel after those days, says the LORD: I will put My law in their minds, and write it on their hearts; and I will be their God, and they shall be My people. (Jer. 31:31–33 NKJV)

The prophets and people waited for the new covenant and watched for their promised Messiah. They groaned under Roman oppression and prayed that God would send deliverance . . . and He heard their prayers. During the Feast of Weeks, fifty days after the Passover Sabbath, the new covenant was written upon the hearts of those willing to receive it.

Let's back up a year or two before that eventful Pentecost

described in the book of Acts. During the time of the Roman Empire, after the building of the second Temple, the Festival of Weeks or Pentecost was a celebration for rejoicing in the successful harvest of two grain crops—barley, which ripened first, and wheat. If you'll recall, the omer, or sheaf of barley, was offered to the Lord at the Feast of Firstfruits, which signified the beginning of the barley harvest. Pentecost marks the completion of the wheat harvest, and was also known as *Yom ha-Bikkurim*, the day of offering the first loaves to God.

> *The* Greek translation of the Bible in the time of the New Testament translated the "fifty days" of Leviticus 23:16 as *pentekosta hemeras*, and so gave rise to the name *Pentecost*.
> —RALPH GOWER

Writer Hayyim Schauss remarks that by the era of the second Temple, during the time of Christ, Pentecost "did not play a great role in the Jewish life. . . . It was obviously a festival observed only in the Temple, and not to any noticeable extent outside of Jerusalem. The holiday first attained importance when it became the festival of the giving of the Torah, of God revealing Himself on Mount Sinai."[2]

The Festival of Weeks, or Pentecost, may not have been as important as Passover, but it was still a pilgrimage festival, and thousands of Jews returned to Jerusalem in order to fulfill the Lord's command. The ancient city was packed with religious pilgrims, and once again the streets rang with the voices and accents of men from every corner of the known world.

Keeping the image of the Hebrews at Sinai in mind, let's look at the story of Pentecost as Luke recorded it in the book of Acts. Nearly every aspect of that Mount Sinai experience was duplicated as 120 faithful followers of Christ gathered in the Upper Room, the site of Jesus' last supper. Ten people, a minyan, was the number required by Jewish law to have a kosher prayer meeting. Ten representatives for the twelve tribes of Israel (totaling 120) huddled together, trying to understand why Jesus had commanded them to "tarry in the city of Jerusalem until you are endued with power from on high" (Luke 24:49 NKJV).

As the followers of Christ prayed in the upstairs room, they joined together in one mind, one heart, and one spirit. Suddenly, Moses' experience on Mount Sinai was reenacted.

A rushing mighty wind filled the Upper Room. Tongues of fire rested on the disciples' heads just as fire rested on the summit of Mount Sinai. Surely many of them realized that this was what Jesus Himself had predicted would happen. Days earlier Jesus had promised His followers, "But you shall receive power when the Holy Spirit has come upon you" (Acts 1:8 NKJV).

Empowerment came in awesome ways. Just as God spoke on Mount Sinai in every known language, even so the disciples began to speak in every known language (Acts 2:6). Those who had been timid were gifted with holy boldness.

The Spirit bestowed gifts upon every man and woman present, creating apostles, prophets, evangelists, pastors, teachers, and organizers.

The giving of the Ten Commandments at Sinai was a rehearsal for the giving of the Holy Spirit at Mount Zion. Notice the parallels:[3]

Shavuot at Mount Sinai	Shavuot upon Mount Zion (in Jerusalem's Upper Room)
Occurred on the fiftieth day after Red Sea	Occurred on the fiftieth day after Firstfruits
Commandments of God were written on tablets of stone	Commandments of God were written on human hearts (Jer. 31:33; 2 Cor. 3:3)
The commandments were written by the finger of God	The commandments were written by the Spirit of God (Heb. 8:10)
Three thousand slain (Ex. 21:1–8, 26–28)	Three thousand born again (Acts 2:38–41)
The letter of the Torah given	The Spirit of the Torah bestowed (Rom. 2:29; 7:6)

The fire and wind and rumbling about Mount Sinai foreshadowed the coming power of Pentecost, and oh, what power it was! Paul proclaimed, "For the kingdom of God is not in word but in power" (1 Cor. 4:20 NKJV). The gospel of the empty tomb is a story of power. Let no one mistake the message. There is power in His name, power in His gospel, power in His blood, and power in His church. If the apostles wanted

to sing a contemporary hymn in the Upper Room, they couldn't have chosen a better one than "All hail the pow'r of Jesus' name! Let angels prostrate fall; bring forth the royal diadem, and crown Him Lord of all!"

Lord and Father God, how we praise You that Your power is available through Your Holy Spirit! Make us channels of blessing, Father, examine us, cleanse us, dedicate us to Your purposes and praise.

Day Three: Present-Day Pentecost

*W*e've already discussed how the date of Pentecost, or Shavuot, shifted from always being on the Sunday fifty days after the Feast of Firstfruits to fifty days after the beginning of Pesach, or Passover. Because of this shift, contemporary Jews always celebrate the holiday on the sixth day of the Hebrew month of Sivan. During this festival, Jewish people celebrate their covenant relationship with God and reaffirm their commitment to a Jewish life of study and practice.

After the destruction of the Temple, the meaning of Pentecost changed somewhat. It is no longer a harvest festival, though evidence of its agricultural roots are still present.

The custom of counting the days from the offering of the *omer* (sheaf of barley) to the offering of two loaves is prescribed in the Bible. The tradition of decorating homes with green leaves and garlands harkens back to the fact that Pentecost originally celebrated a bountiful harvest.

The tradition of staying awake all of Pentecost eve is said to go back to the days of Moses and Mount Sinai. According to a midrashic story, God made Himself manifest on Sinai at noon, but the children of Israel were still asleep at the time, so Moses had to go to their tents to wake them. Therefore, Jews stay awake on Shavuot eve to demonstrate that there will be no need to rouse them to receive the word of God.

Contemporary Jewish families gather the night before Pentecost for an all-night Torah study session called *tikkun leil Shavuot*. During the night hours, passages from Ruth and the

Pentateuch (the first five books of the Bible) are read to commemorate God's giving of the Ten Commandments to Israel.

Another ritual associated with Pentecost involves eating dairy foods such as cheese blintzes and cheesecake. Rabbinic tradition draws an analogy between the sweetness and nourishment the Jew receives from milk and honey to the sweetness and nourishment of the words of Torah—the Bible.[4] Others explain the dairy tradition by stating that after the children of Israel received the Ten Commandments from Moses, they were so tired and hungry they could not wait for the women to prepare a meal of meat, so they rushed to eat whatever dairy products were at hand.[5] David C. Gross, a Jewish writer, offers yet another explanation for the custom: "We eat dairy products in order to put away our shame that our ancestors worshiped the golden calf, which incited Moses to smash the first set of Ten Commandments in disgust."[6]

Not all Feast of Pentecost rituals are ancient. The ceremony of confirmation, added in the nineteenth century, commemorates the maturation of boys and girls. In years past families brought the firstfruits of their harvest to the Temple; today parents bring their children to the synagogue to participate in confirmation. Jewish religious leaders saw Shavuot as a natural day to confirm young people because Pentecost is regarded as the holiday in which all Jewish people confirm their faith. Selections from the book of Ruth, read in the synagogue, remind the listeners that Ruth, a Gentile, accepted the God of Israel.

Time and time again in the Old Testament Scriptures, God demanded the best from His people. We are not to give Him the dregs of our lives—the leftover time, snippets of effort, or "extra" money. We are to give Him of the firstfruits of our increase—the first tithe of our income, our most excellent

efforts, our most earnest devotion. God doesn't want the things you begrudge Him—He wants your best.

Because that's what you give someone you truly love.

Give of your best to the Master;
Give of the strength of your youth;
Throw your soul's fresh, glowing ardor
Into the battle for truth.
—Howard Grose

Day Four: Pentecost in Prophecy

*N*otice how the offering of Pentecost differs from that of Firstfruits: The people were to bring two loaves of bread, baked with leaven, not a sheaf of separate grain. This offering points toward the unity of Jew and Gentile established by the advent of the Holy Spirit at Pentecost.

During Passover and the Feast of Unleavened Bread, all yeast products, representing sin, were to be totally avoided and put away. Why, then, would God command that these loaves be made with leaven?

Passover and the Feast of Unleavened Bread point to Jesus, our Savior who was without sin. Pentecost, however, points toward the congregation of Israel and the church of Jesus Christ. We are, regrettably, still clothed in mortal bodies and prone to sin. Until we inherit our supernatural resurrection bodies we will be clothed in sinful flesh. So the loaves used at the Feast of Pentecost are made with leaven.

In the Bible, the number two is the number of witness and agreement. For example, the Bible tells us that two witnesses establish a truth (Matt. 18:19–20; John 5:31–33). The Bible is a book of twos:

- "No man can serve two masters" (Matt. 6:24 KJV). Mark Twain said this verse proves polygamy will never work!
- "A certain man had two sons" (Luke 15:11 NKJV): The prodigal son, who represents the sins of the flesh, and

the elder brother, who represents the sins of the spirit. Both were equal in their sin before God.

- There are two covenants—one given in the Old Testament, one in the New Testament.
- Over and over again in Scripture, there are only two positions for individuals to choose between: saved or lost, wheat or tares, sheep or goats, heaven or hell, light or darkness, a servant of Christ or a slave to Satan and sin.

The Ten Commandments were inscribed upon two stones at Sinai, and the Ten Commandments may be fulfilled by obeying two: "Jesus said to him, '"You shall love the LORD your God with all your heart, with all your soul, and with all your mind." This is the first and great commandment. And the second is like it: "You shall love your neighbor as yourself." On these two commandments hang all the Law and the Prophets'" (Matt. 22:37–40 NKJV).

Together the congregation of Israel and the congregation of believers in Jesus are chosen by God and holy to Him. Please understand—I am not saying that every Jewish person or every church member is automatically going to heaven. *Each individual* must make his own decision about accepting Jesus Christ as Savior. But there is no denying the fact that Israel and the church are both beloved by our Lord. The two loaves of Pentecost represent these very special entities.

Before returning to heaven after His resurrection, Jesus told His disciples that He would send a Helper who would continue His ministry: "And I will pray the Father, and He will give you another Helper, that He may abide with you

forever—the Spirit of truth, whom the world cannot receive, because it neither sees Him nor knows Him; but you know Him, for He dwells with you and will be in you" (John 14:16–17 NKJV).

Jesus promised that the Holy Spirit would not only be *with* the disciples, but would actually dwell *in* them, a constant, comforting presence. He told them to wait in Jerusalem for the One who would come:

> And being assembled together with them, He com-manded them not to depart from Jerusalem, but to wait for the Promise of the Father, "which," He said, "you have heard from Me; for John truly baptized with water, but you shall be baptized with the Holy Spirit not many days from now. . . . But you shall receive power when the Holy Spirit has come upon you; and you shall be witnesses to Me in Jerusalem, and in all Judea and Samaria, and to the end of the earth." (Acts 1:4–5, 8 NKJV)

Given our natural inclination to commemorate and cele-brate birthdays, we really ought to throw the church a party on Pentecost. A number of significant events occurred on that day:

At Pentecost, the promised holy Comforter descended to indwell believers (John 16:7–8). The followers of Christ were gathered together in expectation, just as the children of Israel were united in heart as they waited to hear the voice of God at Sinai.

At Pentecost, the Spirit's gifts were abundantly outpoured upon the Jews first, then upon Gentiles (Acts 10:45). Just as Ruth accepted the God of Israel and so was blessed by Him, so all the Gentiles who heard and accepted Peter's preaching were filled with the Holy Spirit.

The church was born at Pentecost (Acts 2:42–47; 5:14). Multitudes of men and women, Jews and Gentiles, free men and slaves, were filled with a common spirit and the same love for the risen Lord. The Church—triumphant, powerful, and transcendent—rose like a glorious beacon, shining light into the dark places in men's hearts.

The first missionaries were born at Pentecost! From that upper room, Jews and Jewish converts went forth to spread the gospel (Acts 2:5). Jesus had promised His followers that they would be witnesses for Him in Jerusalem, Judea, Samaria, and the uttermost parts of the earth, and Pentecost presented the perfect opportunity to spread the Word! The city of Jerusalem was filled with devout people from all over the earth, and those who believed carried the message of the gospel back to their homes.

At Pentecost, the gospel was proclaimed to every nationality and race in their own tongue (Acts 2:4–11). Oh, I wish I could have been present to see Cretans and Arabs and Egyptians and Libyans hearing the wonderful news! Those who spilled out of the Upper Room weren't babbling nonsense, they were telling the wonderful works of God to anyone who would listen. These common, uneducated men spoke in every known language, so every passerby could hear the truth of the gospel!

At Pentecost, three thousand were converted by a single sermon (Acts 2:37–41). Keep in mind, friend, that Peter's sermon wasn't televised, tape-recorded, or transmitted. Impetuous Peter, the disciple who had been afraid to claim Christ only a few weeks before, stood in a clearing and proclaimed the truth in a loud voice. He didn't pull any punches or try to sanitize his message—he spoke the truth boldly and without apology, and three thousand recognized the truth in his words.

At Pentecost, Joel's prophecy about Pentecost was fulfilled (Joel 2:28–32; Acts 2:16–21). Peter himself quoted from the prophet Joel, testifying to the fact that the Spirit had been poured out upon God's servants. His prophetic stopwatch—the seventy weeks described in Daniel's vision—had come to a halt, for these were the last days, a time of grace when whoever calls upon the name of the Lord shall be saved (Acts 2:21).

But God's stopwatch will begin running again soon, my friend. He waits because He is merciful toward us. "The Lord is not slack concerning His promise, as some count slackness, but is longsuffering toward us, not willing that any should perish but that all should come to repentance" (2 Peter 3:9 NKJV).

The LORD sat enthroned at the Flood,
And the LORD sits as King forever.
The LORD will give strength to His people;
The LORD will bless His people with peace.
—Psalm 29:10–11 NKJV

Day Five: Pentecost Made Personal

*T*he purpose of pentecostal power is evangelism. "But you shall receive power when the Holy Spirit has come upon you; and you shall be witnesses to Me" (Acts 1:8 NKJV). The top priority of every Christian is to be a soul winner, and Solomon assured us that "he who wins souls is wise" (Prov. 11:30 NKJV). The first evidence of supernatural power is soul winning. Without that, Christians are like trees without fruit, wells without water, and clouds without rain.

The Bible teacher Harold Willmington makes a great point in his book *The King Is Coming*. According to Willmington, the story of Pentecost contains a very practical and prophetic truth:

> According to Acts 2, the first convert was added to the body of Christ at Pentecost. What an occasion that must have been, with 3,000 answering Peter's "altar call"! And God had provided 120 "personal workers" to deal with them (Acts 1:15, 2:1 NKJV). We know that God himself keeps all records. Perhaps someday at the judgment seat of Christ one of these 120 will hear the Master say: "Well done, thou good and faithful servant. You led the first individual into that spiritual body!"
>
> If this be true, and if Christ's coming is at hand, it is entirely possible that a soul-winner reading these very words might one day hear similar words from Jesus: "Well done, thou good and faithful servant. You led the *last* individual

into that spiritual body!" At any rate, someday a soul-winner will point some seeking sinner to the Savior and it will be all over![7]

What will Jesus say when *you* stand before the Savior?

I'd like to mention one final picture found in the Festival of Pentecost. Just as the giving of the Law was a rehearsal for the giving of the Spirit, the entire Pentecost experience is part of our "wedding rehearsal" for the marriage of the Lamb. When you accepted Christ and were baptized by His Spirit, you became betrothed to the Lamb.

The image of a wedding is often used in Scripture. Typically, an ancient Hebrew wedding took place in two stages: The first stage was the betrothal, during which the bride and groom were legally joined, though they did not live

together. The written betrothal contract was called a *ketubah*, and could not be broken without a legal divorce, a *get*.

You may recall from the Christmas story that Mary and Joseph were betrothed when she became pregnant with Jesus. Alarmed at the thought that his bride-to-be was carrying another man's child, Joseph was tempted to quietly obtain a divorce until an angel spoke to him in a dream and told him that Mary carried the Son of God.

The second stage of a Hebrew wedding is the consummation of the marriage. The groom prepares a place for his bride, then journeys to her father's house to get her. Amid great rejoicing, the groom returns with his bride, calls his friends, and arranges for a festive wedding supper.

Jeremiah 2:2–3 tells us that at Mount Sinai, God betrothed Himself to Israel:

> I remember you,
> The kindness of your youth,
> The love of your betrothal,
> When you went after Me in the wilderness,
> In a land that was not sown.
> Israel was holiness to the LORD,
> The firstfruits of His increase. (NKJV)

The Torah, or teaching, which God gave to Israel at Mount Sinai was a betrothal contract. Just as marriage is a covenant, or an agreement between two people, even so the words that Moses wrote formed a marriage covenant between God and Israel:

> And Moses wrote all the words of the LORD. And he rose early in the morning, and built an altar at the foot of the

mountain, and twelve pillars according to the twelve tribes of Israel. . . . Then he took the Book of the Covenant and read in the hearing of the people. And they said, "All that the LORD has said we will do, and be obedient." And Moses took the blood, sprinkled it on the people, and said, "This is the blood of the covenant which the LORD has made with you according to all these words." (Ex. 24:4, 7–8 NKJV)

But when Moses came down from the mountain, the newly betrothed nation of Israel had already forsaken her first love. Her leaders were dancing around the image of a golden calf; her love had already eroded to unfaithfulness. In a fit of righteous anger, Moses threw down the stone tablets upon which God Himself had written, breaking the record of a covenant with Israel (Ex. 32:15–19).

God did renew the covenant with Israel (Ex. 34:10–28), but Moses, not God, wrote upon the second set of stones. The bride's fickle heart interrupted the "wedding rehearsal," but God's love is an enduring love. As we will see next week, the wedding plans are still valid.

Christians are betrothed to Christ through the new covenant written on our hearts and sanctified by the blood of Christ. We love a heavenly Groom we have not seen, and believe He may come at any moment.

Today the Master's Son, Jesus Christ, waits to come for His bride. When He comes to fetch her away, anyone who has trusted Him, Jew or Gentile, will go with Him to the place He has prepared. If you are a believer in Christ, a place at the wedding supper is reserved for you.

But we can't become so heavenly focused that we forget one important fact: The purpose of Pentecost is evangelism.

Pentecostal power was given so that you can be a witness for Christ in *your* Jerusalem, *your* Judea, and *your* Samaria.

How can you be a faithful witness tomorrow? Every person God brings across your path is a divine appointment; there are no "coincidences" for a believer. And soon, very soon, someone like you will lead that *last* soul to Christ before His return . . .

"Do you not say," asked Jesus, "'There are still four months and then comes the harvest'? Behold, I say to you, lift up your eyes and look at the fields, for they are already white for harvest!" (John 4:35 NKJV).

The fields are white, my friend. Thrust in the sickle and let's bring in the harvest. Someone won you to Christ . . . who will you win?

Father God, help us to walk worthy of the vocation to which You have called us. You called us to be witnesses, to be Your arms of love, Your ministering hands, Your faithful prophets. Remind us to proclaim Your gospel as You give the opportunity, and open our eyes to the people You bring across our paths.

The Feasts of the Latter Rain

PART

Two

The Feast
of Trumpets

SEPTEMBER 11
1999

SEPTEMBER 30
2000

SEPTEMBER 18
2001

SEPTEMBER 7
2002

SEPTEMBER 27
2003

SEPTEMBER 16
2004

OCTOBER 4
2005

Day One: The Feast of Trumpets

While the first four festivals occur in close proximity, an entire season passes before the fall commemoration of trumpets begins. This long period between the spring and fall feasts represents the dispensation of grace in which we now live. Of all the feasts, this is the only time span in prophecy that cannot be exactly determined. The incalculable period is the time between Christ's death and His return. It is the time when we wait for the angels to blow God's great trumpet that will call the bride of Christ to her mansions on high.

> Then the LORD spoke to Moses, saying, "Speak to the children of Israel, saying: 'In the seventh month, on the first day of the month, you shall have a sabbath-rest, a memorial of blowing of trumpets, a holy convocation. You shall do no customary work on it; and you shall offer an offering made by fire to the LORD.'" (Lev. 23:23–25 NKJV)

The Feast of Trumpets, now more commonly known as *Rosh Hashanah* (Hebrew for "head of the year"), is the first day of the Jewish civil year. Rosh Hashanah begins on the first day of the seventh month, Tishri (September or October on the English calendar). This festival is also known as the Day of Judgment, when God sits on His throne and determines the destiny of each individual in the year ahead. According to Jewish tradition, this is the date on which God created Adam, the first man. Because the first Hebrew words of the book of

Genesis, "in the beginning" read "on the first of Tishri" when turned around, Rosh Hashanah is known as the birthday of the world.[1]

In order to show their trust in God's compassion, Jews dress in their best for the festival and celebrate with quiet joy. White, signifying purity, is the favorite color. The Torah is covered in white fabric throughout the holidays, and the *kittel*, a white smocklike garment worn over other clothes, is often seen in the synagogue. Because the spotless kittel resembles a burial shroud, it reminds the people of man's mortality as well as purity.

If you've seen Mr. Spock give a split-fingered Vulcan salute on reruns of *Star Trek,* you have also seen the traditional sign used by the Kohanim, the Jewish priestly class, to bless the congregation on Rosh Hashanah. The priests raise their hands and allow a V-shaped gap between their third and fourth fingers to form "windows" through which God can send His blessings. The blessing is usually given as part of the benediction at the Rosh Hashanah service.[2]

The *shofar*, a curved ram's horn, is blown to awaken sinners and to confuse Satan, who, it is believed, will therefore be unable to act in his role as accuser of Israel.[3] The shofar has always held a prominent role in the history of Israel. The shofar sounded when the Torah was given to Israel (Ex. 19:19), and it was the instrument used when the walls of Jericho fell (Josh.

6:20). Gideon had his men blow the shofar in order to frighten the Midianites (Judg. 7:16–22), and Zechariah prophesied that Israel will be advised of the advent of the Messiah at the sound of the shofar (Zech. 9:14–16). The shofar was blown at the beginning of the year of Jubilee (Lev. 25:9), and to announce the start of festivals (Num. 10:10). The shofar was blown during the coronation of kings (1 Kings 1:34, 39), and seven shofroth will be sounded when God judges the earth during the Tribulation (Rev. 8–9).[4]

The trumpets of God are the most important signal the world can possibly receive. Rosh Hashanah is a picture of the rapture of the church, an event that is drawing very near.

In 1 Corinthians 15:51–52, Paul wrote, "Behold, I tell you a mystery: We shall not all sleep, but we shall all be changed—in a moment, in the twinkling of an eye, at the last trumpet. For the trumpet will sound, and the dead will be raised incorruptible, and we shall be changed." This mass ingathering of believers, the bride of Christ, is commonly called the Rapture.

Paul explained the mystery of the Rapture, the next event on God's prophetic calendar. At the sound of God's trumpet, believers who have died will come out of the grave to be raised incorruptible, with new, supernatural, immortal bodies. Those who have not yet died a physical death will also be instantly changed and caught up in the clouds to meet Jesus Christ.

Great confusion exists in Christian circles over the meaning of the "last trumpet" Paul mentioned. Some theologians reason that if there is a *last* trumpet there has to be a series of trumpets. The only series of trumpets mentioned in the New Testament is described in Revelation 8–9, so these theologians surmise that the church will go through the Great Tribulation.

No, my friend. If there is a series of trumpets, I believe it

will come from the trumpet that will sound forth on Rosh Hashanah! A shofar is sounded in three ways—sounds known as *tekiah*, *shevarim*, and *truah*—but one distinguishing feature of the Jewish celebration is the last, climactic blast, known as the *Tekiah Gedolah*. This is not the usual series of short bursts, indicating alarm, but a long blast, signaling victory. I believe this last blast is the "last trumpet" to which Paul referred.

In explaining His return, Jesus left us with a paradox. On one hand, He said, "But of that day and hour no one knows, not even the angels of heaven, but My Father only" (Matt. 24:36 NKJV). On the other hand, we *can* know that He "is near—at the doors!" (Matt. 24:33 NKJV).

How can we know that He is near? We find a clue in Matthew 24:38–39: "For as in the days before the flood, they were eating and drinking, marrying and giving in marriage, until the day that Noah entered the ark, and did not know until the flood came and took them all away, so also will the coming of the Son of Man be" (NKJV).

Noah lived in a situation very similar to ours. God had issued a warning, a call to repentance, and He had told Noah to prepare and be ready. Noah obeyed. Even though he didn't know the exact time the Flood would come, he knew it was near, even at the door, because God put him, his family, and the animals on the boat and personally closed that door. Noah didn't know the exact moment the rains would fall and the fountains of the deep would be opened, but he knew without any doubt that the time was near.

From signs of Bible prophecy, such as those detailed in my book *Beginning of the End,* we know the end is near. Without a doubt, we are the terminal generation.

When will the rapture of the church take place? I believe it

may happen at the Feast of Trumpets. Pray up! Pack up! Look up! We're going up in the twinkling of an eye.

Father God, in the Old Testament the trump of God was used to summon Your people to battle and to worship. I praise You, Father, that the trumpet call of the Rapture will summon Your angels to clear the way for us to ascend with You, even as Your trump calls us to worship You in beauty and holiness. Help us to be ready, Lord. Help us to live each moment of this day as if the trump could sound at any moment.

Day Two: Trumpets in the Time of Christ

*T*he Feast of Trumpets was not known as Rosh Hashanah or the beginning of a new year prior to the Jews' Babylonian captivity. In Leviticus 23:24 and Numbers 29:1, God commanded the people to observe the first day of the seventh month as a holy day, but He never designated it as the first day of the new year. If you're wondering how the first day of the seventh month could possibly mark the beginning of a new year, you need to understand that the Jewish calendar is built on two cycles. Just as some businesses operate on a fiscal calendar that begins and ends on a month other than January, the Jewish religious calendar begins in the spring, while the civil calendar begins with Tishri in the fall.

Because God decreed that the seventh day and the seventh year are holy, it is logical that the seventh month would be holy too. "It is worthy of note," writes Hayyim Schauss, "that the Bible does not refer to the day as the New Year; neither do any Jewish books written in the period of the second Temple. We must, however, take it for granted that about the time of the destruction of the second Temple [A.D. 70] the day was observed as the New Year. For in the literature of the Tannaim, which dates to the years shortly after the destruction, the first of Tishri is called Rosh Hashanah."[5]

Through the ages, whether the Feast of Trumpets was associated with the New Year or not, the shofar was blown in the synagogue, and the thoughts of the Jewish people turned toward God. Rosh Hashanah is known in the Bible as *Yom*

Teruah, the Day of the Awakening Blast. It is believed that Psalms 93–100 were composed for the Feast of Trumpets.

The Bible does not specifically record the story of a Feast of Trumpets during Christ's lifetime, but it does describe one held after the Babylonian captivity. As God granted His people permission to return to the promised land, Nehemiah and Ezra, the godly priest, gathered the people together and taught them about the festival God had established for the first day of the seventh month:

> So Ezra the priest brought the Law before the assembly of men and women and all who could hear with understanding on the first day of the seventh month. Then he read from it in the open square that was in front of the Water Gate from morning until midday, before the men and women and those who could understand; and the ears of all the people were attentive to the Book of the Law . . . And Nehemiah, who was the governor, Ezra the priest and scribe, and the Levites who taught the people said to all the people, "This day is holy to the LORD your God; do not mourn nor weep." For all the people wept, when they heard the words of the Law.
>
> Then he said to them, "Go your way, eat the fat, drink the sweet, and send portions to those for whom nothing is prepared; for this day is holy to our Lord. Do not sorrow, for the joy of the LORD is your strength." . . . And all the people went their way to eat and drink, to send portions and rejoice greatly, because they understood the words that were declared to them. (Neh. 8:2–3, 9–10, 12 NKJV)

The Jews who heard Ezra wept because they had not heard the Law during their lifetimes. They had recently

returned from exile in Babylon, and undoubtedly many of them had forgotten the Lord their God. Guilt struck their consciences; and they wept because they recognized their sin and repented of it.

Nehemiah wisely told the people not to weep, but to rejoice. God had brought them back to their promised land; He had brought them back to Himself. The day was therefore holy, and cause for rejoicing.

David the psalmist wrote, "With trumpets and the sound of a horn; Shout joyfully before the LORD, the King" (Ps. 98:6 NKJV); and "Blessed are the people who know the joyful sound!" (Ps. 89:15 NKJV). It is important for every person to hear the sound of the shofar.

In Old Testament days, the shofar was used only on solemn occasions. The voice of the shofar was so strong at Sinai that all the people who heard it trembled. The shofar was also sounded when war was waged upon a dangerous enemy. The Jews believe that the shofar not only wakes them from sleep, but reminds them of duty to follow God's Law and wage war against Satan.

Rosh Hashanah, celebrated on the first day of the seventh month, begins a period known as the Days of Awe, or *Yomin Noroim*. These special days end with *Yom Kippur* (Hebrew for "day of covering"), which falls upon the tenth day of Tishri (September or October on the English calendar). In practice, Rosh Hashanah and Yom Kippur are unique festivals, quite unlike the others celebrated by the Jews. They are not associated with nature or harvests, nor are they supposed to be times of jubilant rejoicing. According to Hayyim Schauss, "They are concerned only with the life of the individual, with his religious feelings and innermost probings. Rosh Hashanah is the Jewish New Year but, in contrast with the

New Year of other peoples, it is greeted not with noise and joy, but with a serious and contrite heart."[6]

> *One* should not exaggerate the tone of [Rosh Hashanah]. It is awe, not terror. There is a strong conviction that God is understanding, merciful, and loving.
> —RABBI IRVING GREENBERG

Samuele Bacchiocchi explains the significance of the holiday:

> In ancient times, the blowing of the trumpets was understood to be a call to repent and prepare oneself to stand trial before God, who would execute His judgment ten days later on the Day of Atonement. The importance of the feast is indicated by the fact that the Jews anticipated its arrival on the first day of each month (new moon) through short blasts of the shofar (Num. 10:10, Ps. 81:3). These short blasts were an anticipation of the long alarm blasts to be sounded on the new moon of the seventh month.[7]

Rosh Hashanah has never been a festival for the home, though a festive meal is eaten afterward. The observance and ceremony take place in the synagogue.

Like those of generations past, today's Rosh Hashanah services begin early in the morning and do not end until midday. "All the prayers are recited," says Schauss, "and chanted with pious fervor."

But there are, in addition, certain exalted moments

when the spirit that fills all hearts on the Days of Awe expands and religious feelings are raised to the highest pitch. Such an exalted moment comes at the blowing of the shofar. Psalm 47 is recited seven times; then all quiets down. The hearts of the worshipers beat fast; and when the trumpeter calls out, "Blessed be," the beginning of the benediction, a tremor of awe and fear passes through the congregation.[8]

Oh, clap your hands, all you peoples!
Shout to God with the voice of triumph! . . .
God has gone up with a shout,
The Lord with the sound of a trumpet.
Sing praises to God, sing praises!
—Psalm 47:1–6 NKJV

Day Three: Present-Day Feast of Trumpets

*T*he customs of the contemporary observance of Rosh Hashanah are designed to help Jews enter into the new year with a new spirit so they might be written down in the Book of Life and Blessing.

Self-examination and repentance are among the customs for this festival. Repentance begins with the recognition of one's faults, failures, and weaknesses, and the willingness to change. Broken relationships are mended; forgiveness is sought from offended friends and relatives.

It is also a custom to give aid to the needy. In many homes, it is the custom to deposit money in a *Tzedakah* box as one comes to the table for the lighting of the candles before dinner.

Jewish families observing Rosh Hashanah often invite guests to their festive dinner. Candles are lit, as they are on the Sabbath, and children are blessed. It is also customary to eat pieces of apple dipped in honey. The apple and honey symbolize the hope for a good and sweet year. After eating, the following prayers are recited: "Lord our God and God of our people, may the new year be good and sweet for us. Blessed are You, O Lord our God, Ruler of the universe, Creator of the fruit of the tree."

Congregational worship is also an important part of contemporary Rosh Hashanah observance. Just as Nehemiah gathered the returning Jews around the Temple gate to hear the Word of God, so contemporary Jews gather in the synagogue to study Torah, pray, and sing together. Of course, this

service includes the sound of the shofar, or ram's horn. Numbers 29:1 teaches, "And in the seventh month, on the first day of the month, you shall have a holy convocation. You shall do no customary work. For you it is a day of blowing the trumpets."

The blowing of the shofar has not been neglected in modern times. Of a Rosh Hashanah service in his synagogue, David Gross writes,

> The sounding of the shofar, the ram's horn, is closely associated with Rosh Hashanah. The overwhelming majority of worshipers who take part in Rosh Hashanah services and who rise to hear the rabbi summon the shofar blower to sound the ancient notes of *tekiah* [a long, clear note], *teruah*, [nine very short notes] and *shevarim* [three short notes] experience an almost mystical passage of time. The shofar's sounds are almost eerie. One listens, wondering whether the shofar sounder will succeed in producing the requisite note. Then when the sounds are emitted, there is a momentary connection with all Jews in all places through the ages, from Mount Sinai on, who have been listening to the same memorable sounds. . . . You cannot adequately describe the awesomeness that envelops people who are in synagogue on Rosh Hashanah when the shofar blasts are heard. The sounds seem to reach out from eons ago to the depths of a person's soul. The theme of the High Holy Days, in which Jews are urged to repent, pray, and perform good deeds, never is felt more deeply than when the shofar blasts reverberate through the synagogue.[9]

Another Rosh Hashanah custom, known as *tashlikh*, involves walking to a nearby river or stream, and emptying

one's pockets into the water. Springing from Micah 7:19 ("you will cast all our sins into the depths of the sea" [NKJV]), the act is meant to symbolize the casting of sins into the sea of forgiveness. Usually just lint makes its way into the water, but occasionally some people put bread crumbs in their pockets to feed the fish.

With every ritual and custom, the Jews are reminded that Rosh Hashanah is a time to wake up and examine oneself before God. The sound of the trumpet alerts them, as it alerts all of us, to the fact that every action has a consequence, and we are responsible for every thought, word, and deed.

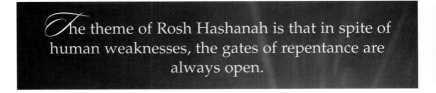

The theme of Rosh Hashanah is that in spite of human weaknesses, the gates of repentance are always open.

The Feast of Trumpets falls near the end of a special forty-day season, *Teshuvah*, beginning on the first day of Elul and ending with Yom Kippur, the Day of Atonement. The Hebrew word *Teshuvah* means to "return or repent," and the message of the season is clear: Repent before the Feast of Trumpets. Don't wait, or you will find yourself unprepared to stand before God.

That message is still valid today, my friends. Over the years, rabbinic tradition began to identify Rosh Hashana as *Yom Hadin*, or Judgment Day. A talmudic parable pictures God sitting in judgment on the world and each individual on this first day of the new year. According to tradition, the Jews believe that three books are opened in heaven—one for the righteous, one for the wicked, and one for those who fall into neither category. God determines the fate of each individual

during the ten days between Rosh Hashanah and Yom Kippur, and so it is customary for Jews to greet one another with the words, "May you be written down for a good year."[10]

"The image of God as judge," writes Peter Knobel, "about to inscribe human beings according to their deeds in the appropriate Book of Life, underscores the Jewish concept of human beings as moral free agents responsible for the choices which they make. We are further encouraged to believe that our fate, and indeed the fate of the entire world, depends upon our every act."[11]

Father God, though I cannot hear the sound of the shofar at this moment, I know that You have called us to repent and remember that the eyes of the Lord see everything. Your ears hear every idle word, Your spirit knows every thought that scampers through our minds. Help us to walk as holy examples of Your children.

Day Four: The Prophecy of Trumpets

*I*n order to understand the meaning behind the Feast of Trumpets, we must understand the Jewish roots of our faith. The mystery of the Rapture is explained in the ancient Jewish wedding ceremony to which we were introduced last week in our study of the Feast of Pentecost. The Feast of Pentecost pictures the betrothal ceremony; and the Feast of Trumpets points to the actual wedding!

Follow closely the nuptial chain of events in a traditional Hebrew wedding:

In the ancient ceremony, the bridegroom or an agent of the bridegroom's father went out in search of a bride. (An example is when Abraham sent his servant to secure a bride for Isaac.) A bride would often agree to the marriage without ever seeing her future groom.

Next, a price would be established for the bride—twenty camels, a dozen silver bracelets, or whatever the groom had to offer. The agreed-upon price was called a *mohar.* The bride and groom were then betrothed and legally bound to each other, though they did not yet live together. A scribe would draw up a *ketubah,* or marriage contract, stating the bride price, the promises of the groom (to honor, support, and live with her), and the rights of the bride.

Finally, the groom would present the bride with gifts. Most grooms today give their brides a ring as evidence of love and commitment, but in ancient times the gift could have been almost anything. If the bride accepted her groom's gifts,

together they shared a cup of wine, the cup of the covenant, and the betrothal was complete. Before leaving her home, however, the groom would tell his bride, "I go to prepare a place for you. If I go, I will return again to you."

The bridegroom then went to his father's house to prepare a *chupah*, or wedding canopy. During the following year or so of betrothal, the bride was consecrated and set apart while she waited for her groom. She enjoyed a *mikvah*, or cleansing bath, to purify her for the coming wedding. She had to make herself ready and she had to *stay* ready, for she had no idea when her groom would return. Often she kept a light burning in the window and an extra jar of oil on hand, lest the bridegroom come in the night and find her unprepared.

No engraved invitations were sent out for the wedding. If people preparing a calendar wanted to reserve a day for the celebration, they had a problem. When the young bridegroom was asked for the date of his wedding, he could only reply, "No man knows except my father." Why? Because he could not go get his bride until the father approved of his son's preparation.

When the groom's father decided everything was in place and released his son to go fetch his bride, the groom arrived with a shout and the blowing of a shofar. Thus announced, the bridegroom took the marriage contract to present to the father of his intended bride. He claimed her as his own and took her to his father's house. His father would be waiting to receive the couple, and then the groom's father would take the hand of the bride and place it in the hand of his son. At that moment, she became his wife. That act was called the *presentation*.

After the presentation, the bridegroom would bring his bride to the bridal chamber he had gone to prepare. There he would introduce her to all the society of his friends who had

heard the trumpet and come to celebrate the marriage at the marriage feast. In 2 Corinthians 11:2, Paul wrote to the church, "For I am jealous for you with godly jealousy. For I have betrothed you to one husband, that I may present you as a chaste virgin to Christ" (NKJV).

What a powerful picture of what God has prepared for us! We are the betrothed bride of Christ, sought by the Holy Spirit and purchased at Calvary with Jesus' precious blood. Paul said, "For you were bought at a price" (1 Cor. 6:20 NKJV). The almighty Father looked down from heaven and accepted the price of our redemption. We, the bride, accepted the Groom and the evidence of His love for us. Our betrothal contract is the Word of God, for it contains every promise our loving Groom has made on our behalf.

We exchanged gifts at our betrothal. When we accepted

Him, Jesus gave us love, commitment, and loyalty. God Himself has given us the Holy Spirit, who has bestowed His own gifts of eternal life, grace, faith, love, joy, peace, long-suffering, kindness, goodness, faithfulness, gentleness, and self-control. Like the bride in her purifying *mikvah*, we have been baptized with water and by the cleansing power of the Holy Spirit (Luke 3:16; Acts 1:5).

In this interim, as we wait between Pentecost and Trumpets, Jesus Christ, our Bridegroom, returned to His Father's house to prepare everything for our arrival. Before He departed this earth, Jesus said, "In My Father's house are many mansions; if it were not so, I would have told you. I go to prepare a place for you. And if I go and prepare a place for you, I will come again and receive you to Myself; that where I am, there you may be also" (John 14:2–3 NKJV).

How do we publicly demonstrate our acceptance of Christ? Just like the bride, each time we take the communion cup and drink the wine we proclaim our wedding vows to our beloved Lord. We demonstrate that we love only Him, that we are loyal to Him, and that we are waiting for Him. Like the eager bride, we keep our lamps burning and strive to be ready, for we don't know when He might come.

Our bridegroom will soon come for us. Make no mistake, we must wait with our ears attuned to hear the trumpet sound.

We're not going into or through the Tribulation. We're going home, to the city where there will be no death, no parting, no sorrow, no sickness. We're going to the city where the Lamb is the Light, to the city where roses never fade, to the city inhabited by Abraham, Isaac, Jacob, and King Jesus.

Father, help us not to be like the foolish virgins who had no oil for their lamps when the bridegroom approached. Help us to be ready, to quiet our hearts and listen for the shofar and the loving sound of the Bridegroom's voice.

Day Five: The Feast of Trumpets Made Personal

*T*he primary function of the Feast of Trumpets is to ask us one question: Are we prepared for the coming of Jesus Christ who shall appear in the clouds of heaven with power and great glory? He shall come when the world least expects it, "as a thief in the night" (1 Thess. 5:2 NKJV).

Just as the blast of the shofar awakens the Jews and urges them to search their deeds and remember their Creator, the blast of the Lord's trumpet will awaken us to the realization that the Bridegroom has come. Are you ready for that sound? If you were to die in the next sixty seconds, would you be ready to meet your heavenly Groom?

What happened in an ancient Hebrew wedding after the bridegroom took his bride home? She stood before him and awaited his appraisal. If she was wise, she had prepared a trunk with her wedding clothes, and she adorned herself in beautiful garments that she had prepared out of love for her bridegroom.

In biblical times the marriage feast was a celebration to honor not the bride, as is our custom, but the bridegroom. All the guests who assembled at the marriage supper were expected to compose poems and sing songs to honor him as they appreciated the beauty and grace of his bride.

The blessed Bridegroom has been presented with a bride, and now He is coming to display the bride to all His friends, not that they might honor the bride, but that they might honor the Bridegroom because of the bride's beauty. Jesus will be

honored, not because of what we are, but because of what He has made us. Writing in Ephesians, Paul refers to this analogy when he wrote that Christ gave Himself for the church so that "He might present her to Himself a glorious church, not having spot or wrinkle or any such thing, but that she should be holy and without blemish" (5:27 NKJV).

We're not holy by nature. We're not holy by practice. But the bride is the Father's love gift to the Son to honor the Son for His obedience to the Father's will. When Jesus, the Bridegroom, is presented with His bride, He will say, "She is beautiful, without spot or wrinkle." He will rejoice to lead her to the marriage banquet.

Imagine this, if you will: The bridegroom takes the bride into his chamber, looks her in the eye, and says, "Now I will take you in to meet all my friends. They will want to praise you and exclaim over your beauty. So look into your trunk and pull out those garments you have prepared for our marriage feast." What would you do if you looked into your hope chest and found nothing? Or if you found only slipshod, poorly prepared garments? You would be embarrassed beyond words before your loving bridegroom, his father, and the assembled witnesses.

Soon after the Rapture, we Christians will stand before the judgment seat (sometimes called the "bema seat") of Christ. While Jesus took the full weight of God's judgment of sin for us, we must still stand before God for a final review of our faithfulness. As the nations of the world rise and fall because of their morality, our personal decisions and actions are creating evidence for the coming judgment on us. We will either receive crowns and commendation or reproof and reprimand. Our garments will either be designed to glorify our Bridegroom, or they will appear as filthy rags. The issue won't

be salvation, because this judgment takes place in heaven with the redeemed. The qualities under examination will be our character and faithfulness.

On display at the bema seat will be five great crowns for loyal and trustworthy servants of Christ. To steadfast believers tested by prison and persecution even to the point of death, God will give a crown of life (Rev. 2:10). A never-fading, never-tarnishing diadem awaits the self-sacrificing pastor-shepherds of the flock (1 Peter 5:2–4). Everyone who ran life's race with patient endurance and perseverance will receive a crown of righteousness (2 Tim. 4:8). Evangelists and soul winners can eagerly anticipate receiving the crown of rejoicing (1 Thess. 2:19–20). Finally, all who overcome will be handed a wonderful victor's crown (1 Cor. 9:25).

Which crown will you wear?

Which of your works will be burned, and which will endure?

Will you take your Bridegroom's arm with the scent of smoke upon you? Or will you join Him, dressed in white, with a glowing crown upon your head? John warns all believers, "Hold fast what you have, that no one may take your crown" (Rev. 3:11 NKJV). Run the race to win!

Let us be glad and rejoice and give Him glory, for the marriage of the Lamb has come, and His wife has made herself ready. And to her it was granted to be arrayed in fine linen, clean and bright, for the fine linen is the righteous acts of the saints. Then he said to me, "Write: 'Blessed are those who are called to the marriage supper of the Lamb!'"
—Revelation 19:7–9 NKJV

The Feast
of $\mathcal{A}$tonement

SEPTEMBER 20
1999

OCTOBER 9
2000

SEPTEMBER 27
2001

SEPTEMBER 16
2002

OCTOBER 6
2003

SEPTEMBER 25
2004

OCTOBER 13
2005

Day One: The Day of Atonement

I must die," the preacher Dwight L. Moody once said, "or get somebody to die for me. If the Bible doesn't teach that, it doesn't teach anything. And that is where the atonement of Jesus Christ comes in."[1]

Moody was right. We would be lost, without hope and without purpose, if Christ had not atoned for our sins.

Let's examine the background of this all-important festival. In Leviticus, God commanded Moses to tell the children of Israel to come together on the tenth day of Tishri, the day of Yom Kippur, for worship, self-examination, reflection, and repentance. Today, as in ancient times, Yom Kippur is the most holy, most sacred day of the Jewish year. In biblical times it was the only occasion when the high priest could enter the Holy of Holies.

> And the LORD spoke to Moses, saying: "Also the tenth day of this seventh month shall be the Day of Atonement. It shall be a holy convocation for you; you shall afflict your souls, and offer an offering made by fire to the LORD. And you shall do no work on that same day, for it is the Day of Atonement, to make atonement for you before the LORD your God. (Lev. 23:26–28 NKJV)

Rosh Hashanah and Yom Kippur together are referred to as the "High Holy Days," but of the two, Yom Kippur is the most serious festival. On this day Jews must consider the fact

that they are sinful, and sin separates them from God. In biblical times, a blood offering had to be given in order to atone for the sins of the priest and of the people.

The word *atonement* means "to cover." The same Hebrew word used to describe the Day of Atonement is used to describe Noah's action when he *pitched* the ark within and without with tar. Just as Noah covered the ark with a substance that would come between him and the judgment waters of the Flood, the blood of the Day of Atonement becomes the saving, sealing agent where sin is ritually covered for another year.[2]

> Then he shall kill the goat of the sin offering, which is for the people, bring its blood inside the veil, do with that blood as he did with the blood of the bull, and sprinkle it on the mercy seat and before the mercy seat. So he shall make atonement for the Holy Place, because of the uncleanness of the children of Israel, and because of their transgressions, for all their sins; and so he shall do for the tabernacle of meeting which remains among them in the midst of their uncleanness. (Lev. 16:15–16 NKJV)

When the high priest had finished with the blood of the slain goat, he stepped out in view of the people and put his hands on the head of the remaining goat.

The Hebrew word for "scapegoat" is *azazel*. When lots were drawn to see which goat would be sacrificed and which would be sent away, two tablets were placed in an urn. The tablets were identical in shape and size, but one was inscribed "For the Lord" and the other "For azazel." The priest drew out the tablets, one with his left hand and one with his right, then turned to the goats and placed the corresponding tablets on their heads. One goat was sacrificed for the Lord, the other

was designated to carry away the sins of the people. Later, the bodies of the sacrificial bull and goat were taken outside the camp where they were burned. The ancient meaning for the word *holocaust* is "conflagration," or burnt offering.

The two goats together were the sin offering. One was slaughtered and offered as a burnt offering; the other was led into the wilderness to die after the high priest cast the sins of Israel upon it. Jesus fulfilled both roles in redemption's plan. He was slaughtered at Calvary and bore our sins after God, our High Priest, placed our sins upon His head.

"Surely He has borne our griefs And carried our sorrows; Yet we esteemed Him stricken, Smitten by God, and afflicted" (Isa. 53:4 NKJV). Think of it! Your iniquity, though Satan himself searches for it, cannot be found. Though you may recall your past sin, it is so completely forgiven God can't remember it (Jer. 31:34). One thing God cannot do is remember sin washed in the blood of Jesus Christ.

When Satan tries to remind you of your past—you remind him of his future!

Heavenly Father, as we begin our study of the Day of Atonement, attune our hearts to see the meaning of this most holy service. Our prayers rise to You like the incense from the priest's golden censer, and we enter Your Holy of Holies with reverence and thanksgiving.

Day Two: Atonement in the Time of Christ

*B*y the era of the second Temple, the Day of Atonement was known as "The Great Day" or simply as "The Day." On this day Jews prayed earnestly that their sins would be forgiven.

Many things had changed since the days when Moses instructed the Israelites about how to observe God's Day of Atonement. The temple into which the high priest entered was no longer a tent, as it had been in Aaron's day, nor was it the beautiful building Solomon had built. The Temple in the time of Christ is known as Herod's Temple, because that king had enlarged and improved the ordinary wood and stone temple built under Zerubbabel's leadership.

Herod's temple was a magnificent edifice. Built of the finest white marble, it glowed in the sun. Several courtyards surrounded it—the courtyard for the Gentiles, the courtyard of the women, the courtyard of the men, the courtyard of the priests. The holy Temple mount rose above a series of broad terraces, and on the uppermost terrace stood the altar. Above the altar rose the House of God, which only priests dared to enter. They entered twice a day for daily services, stepping into a long room with walls plated in solid gold. The only light came from a golden menorah, in which seven oil wicks softly glowed. Opposite the menorah stood a golden table bearing twelve loaves of showbread. Beneath these two objects stood the golden altar on which incense was burned twice each day.[3]

Beyond this outer room within the House of God lay the

Holy of Holies, a place so sacred that only the high priest could enter, and only one day per year . . . on Yom Kippur. The holiest place was separated from the rest of a temple by a drape, or veil. By the time of Christ, the only object in the room was a stone, "three fingers high," called the *foundation stone*. The ark of the covenant had been absent for generations.

On the day prior to Yom Kippur, the high priest stood at the eastern gate of the Temple early in the morning. The animals that were to be sacrificed were brought to him for examination. Not only did they have to be perfect and without blemish, but the two goats had to be virtually identical in size and value.

Throughout Jerusalem, the Jews prepared themselves, asking forgiveness of those they had wronged, and reconciling themselves to relatives and friends. Just before Yom Kippur eve, as the sun was about to set, the Jews indulged in a huge feast in order to prepare for the hours of fasting ahead.

As soon as the first ray of dawn crowned the hilly horizon, other priests escorted the high priest to the bathhouse, where he bathed and ceremonially washed his hands and feet ten times. Dressed in his golden robes, he offered the morning sacrifice in full view of the people. With his golden diadem on his head, a plethora of spangled gems on his breast, and golden bells hanging on the hem of his rich purple robe, he must have been a breathtaking sight. After offering the regular daily sacrifice, he was conducted to the bathhouse again, where he washed and dressed in elegant garments of spotless white linen, as God had commanded.

Stepping outside, adorned this time in simple white, he approached the young bull destined for sacrifice. He placed his hands on the bull's head and said: "I beseech Thee, O

Lord! I have sinned, I have been iniquitous, I have transgressed against Thee, I and my household . . ."

After praying over the bull, the priest moved to the two goats, which were tethered on the eastern side of the altar, nearer the congregation. He reached into the urn and shuffled the two golden tablets, ready to draw lots to determine which animal would be the scapegoat, and which would be sacrificed to the Lord.

The people believed it was a good omen if the tablet marked "For the Lord" was drawn out by the priest's right hand, but from A.D. 30 to the destruction of the Temple in A.D. 70—and for those forty years only—the high priest drew the "For azazel" tablet with his right hand.[4] When the scapegoat's tablet was discovered in the priest's right hand, the troubled people fell to their faces in prayer for their Temple and their people.

Once the tablets were drawn, the priest placed them upon the heads of the goats standing before him, sealing their fates. As the sacrificial goat was led away, the high priest tied a red sash on the horns of the azazel goat. For a few quiet moments, the doomed scapegoat faced the assembled congregation who stared at him and waited. He could not be driven out—the people's sin could not be removed—until after the blood was shed.

The priest then returned to the bull, prayed over him again, then killed the animal. The blood was gathered in a basin, and held by another priest while the high priest poured handfuls of incense into a golden ladle. With the ladle in one hand, he picked up a golden fire-pan loaded with burning coals and stepped into the Holy of Holies. Once inside, he placed the fire-pan upon the foundation stone, then poured the incense over the coals. As the Holy of Holies filled with

smoke, he stepped out, prayed again, and took the basin of blood from a priest who had been stirring it to prevent coagulation. Again he entered the Holy of Holies, this time to sprinkle the blood on the altar seven times. He stepped out again, killed the sacrificial goat, collected the blood, and entered the Holy of Holies for a third and final time.

When the priests returned from inside the Most Holy Place, a specially appointed goat-handler took the crimson sash from the goat's horns, tore it in two, and retied one half to the goat's horns. As the people chanted, "Hurry and go," the handler led the condemned animal through a gate of the Temple. In the same manner that we have seen Olympic runners pass a torch, different individuals escorted the goat-handler from point to point until the scapegoat reached the appointed place, a cliff about ten miles outside the city. The goat-handler pushed the animal off the cliff and into the ravine below, and thus the people's sins were eradicated. Runners quickly carried the news back to the Temple.

According to Eddie Chumney, the *Mishnah* mentions an interesting tradition about the scapegoat: "A portion of the crimson sash was attached to the door of the Temple before the goat was sent into the wilderness. The sash would turn from red to white as the goat met its end, signaling to the people that God had accepted their sacrifices and their sins were forgiven . . . The *Mishnah* tells us that 40 years before the destruction of the Temple, the sash stopped turning white. This, of course, was when *Yeshua* [Jesus] was slain on the tree."[5]

I don't know how much of that story is truth and how much is oral tradition, but God does tell us that though our sins be as scarlet, after forgiveness, they shall be as white as snow (Isa. 1:18). And isn't it interesting that the *Mishna*, a book

written by Jewish rabbis, would confirm the time of Jesus' death on the cross?

My friend, Jesus is our High Priest and our Sacrifice for sin. The exercise of animal sacrifice could not in itself bring the forgiveness of sins, for sins can only be forgiven by God. The sacrifices were only pictures, or shadows, of what was to come. We can be forgiven only through the sacrifice of Jesus Christ. Because we have been atoned by Christ's sacrificial offering, we are free to venture into the Holy of Holies whenever we like.

When Jesus lifted up His head on Calvary and cried, "It is finished," the curtain hanging around the Holy of Holies was ripped by an unseen Hand, from top to bottom (Matt. 27:51). The symbolic tearing of the curtain (which Josephus tells us was four inches thick!) signaled that a new avenue to God had been established. Through Jesus Christ, our High Priest and sacrificial Lamb, we can venture into the presence of God without a human mediator. No longer do we have need of a temple, sacrifices, or designated priests. We have the Holy Spirit in our hearts, Jesus as our Mediator, and a heavenly Father who knows our needs even before we do!

And now my head shall be lifted up above my enemies all around me;
Therefore I will offer sacrifices of joy in His tabernacle;
I will sing, yes, I will sing praises to the LORD.
—Psalm 27:6 NKJV

Day Three: Present-Day Atonement

*T*he Temple's destruction in A.D. 70 brought an end to Yom Kippur sacrifices and many of its rituals, but the Day of Atonement lost none of its significance for the Jews. Yom Kippur ends the ten days of penitence that begin with Rosh Hashanah. During these ten days, which is a more intense time of repentance than the month of Elul, in which repentance begins, Jews may participate in penitential rituals such as the *kapparot* ceremony in which money—or a fowl—is sacrificed to atone for sins. Others may participate in a *mikvah*, in which "living" water from a spring or rain is gathered and used for purification. Still others endure *Malkus*, a symbolic ceremony of being flogged for sins.

Nearly all observant Jews will fast on Yom Kippur. Three times the Bible commands the children of Israel to "afflict their souls" or practice self-denial, so one of the most basic practices of Yom Kippur is a twenty-five-hour fast. After eating a large meal before sunset on the night on which the Day of Atonement begins, the Yom Kippur candles are lit, signaling the beginning of the fast period and the beginning of the Day. (Remember: According to the Jewish calendar, a day begins with sunset on the day before.)

After lighting the candles on Yom Kippur eve, Jews will go to the synagogue for the evening service. Men and women may be dressed in white, the color of purity, and very observant Jews may be wearing tennis shoes, having put away leather because it is considered a symbol of war. The story of

Jonah, a man who learned that he could not escape from God, will be read at some point during the Yom Kippur services.

The services continue the next morning and afternoon. At the conclusion of the Yom Kippur services, as the sun sets and a new night begins, seven times the congregation repeats, "The Lord alone is God!" At the end of *neilah*, the concluding prayers of Yom Kippur, the shofar sounds again.

The sound of this *shofar* is special. According to scholar Eddie Chumney, there are three primary *shofroth* (trumpets) to the Jewish people. These three trumpets are associated with specific days of the year. They are the *first trump*, associated with Pentecost, the *last trump*, associated with Rosh Hashanah, and the *great trump*, associated with Yom Kippur.

But Yom Kippur's acts of sacrifice and restitution cannot atone for sin. The author of Hebrews reminded his readers that Old Testament Law required the shedding of blood:

> For when Moses had spoken every precept to all the people according to the law, he took the blood of calves and goats, with water, scarlet wool, and hyssop, and sprinkled both the

book itself and all the people, saying, "This is the blood of the covenant which God has commanded you." Then likewise he sprinkled with blood both the tabernacle and all the vessels of the ministry. And according to the law almost all things are purged with blood, and without shedding of blood there is no remission [of sin]." (Heb. 9:19–22 NKJV)

As Christians, our assurance rests not on anything *we* have done, but on what Christ did for us. Our redemption was purchased by the shed blood of the Lamb of God.

Thank You, heavenly Father, for sending Your Son to shed His precious blood as our atonement. His blood gives eternal life, it brings redemption, it covers us, it justifies us, it grants us forgiveness, it provides cleansing, it reconciles us to God, and enables us to overcome the world. Blessed be the name of Jesus!

Day Four: The Prophecy of Atonement

*M*y friend, I want you to know that I expect Jesus Christ to appear twice in the days ahead—the first time only for an instant in the clouds of glory to protect the Church, His bride, from the wrath of the Tribulation by removing her from the earth before it begins. But He will appear on earth a second time as well, and it is consistent with Scripture to say that Christ's second coming could very well be at Yom Kippur.

Jesus Christ will step down from heaven and place His foot on the Mount of Olives. He will win the battle at Armageddon for Jerusalem and Israel. In the aftermath of this battle, His people will finally understand who He really is and what He has come to offer them. The hearts of the Jewish people—warmed toward God because of His intervention to defeat their enemies, will now turn fully to their true God. And in that moment, the blindness of the Jewish people toward their Messiah will be taken away and they will be saved.

Daniel knew how extremely significant the Day of Atonement would be in God's plan for the future. In Daniel 9:24, the prophet recorded the significance of the sixth feast:

> Seventy weeks are determined
> For your people and for your holy city [Jerusalem],
> To finish the transgression,
> To make an end of sins,
> To make reconciliation for iniquity [Yom Kippur],

To bring in everlasting righteousness,
To seal up vision and prophecy,
And to anoint the Most Holy [Jesus Christ]. (NKJV)

Just as the Crucifixion corresponded to the fulfillment of Passover down to the last detail, the Scripture points to the incredible promise of what will happen on this day, the second coming of Christ. Which Yom Kippur will signal His return?

The second coming of Jesus Christ—and I'm not talking about the Rapture, where Jesus appears in the clouds without touching the earth—should occur 2,520 days, or seven prophetic years of 360 days, after the day Israel signs a seven-year peace accord with the Antichrist. The treaty signing will come after this extraordinary man emerges as the predomi-

nant leader of the European Union or a country or confederacy that was once part of the Roman Empire. He will be the Beast described in Revelation 13:1, the creature who rises from the sea with "seven heads and ten horns, and on his horns ten crowns, and on his heads a blasphemous name" (NKJV). Ten crowns with seven heads of state indicate that three nations of the confederation have fallen under his control.

Although Israel will consider this thoroughly evil man to be the Messiah, he will be Hitler reborn. His reign of evil influence will end, however, when Jesus Christ comes to destroy him. He will fulfill the intent of Yom Kippur, the day of reconciliation between God and His chosen people.

If you'll recall from our readings last week, the Feast of Trumpets points to the Rapture, when the Bride of Christ—all believers—will go to be with Him. The Messiah and His bride will leave their bridal chamber and prepare to come back to earth.

Their return is a matter of some urgency. There's a threat looming outside Jerusalem, for the nations are lining up to make war against the Holy City, and Israel's people are literally quaking with fear. Before we can celebrate the Messiah's return, the Lord Jesus will have to destroy Israel's enemies. He will descend to the earth, placing His feet upon the Mount of Olives. The earth will quake, the nations will tremble, and the Lord and His saints will proceed to Armageddon, where He will destroy Satan and the best of the world's armies, leaders, and governments with a single word.

Then Israel will look upon her Messiah with recognition.

> And I will pour on the house of David and on the inhabitants of Jerusalem the Spirit of grace and supplication; then they will look on Me whom they pierced. Yes, they will

mourn for Him as one mourns for his only son, and grieve for Him as one grieves for a firstborn. In that day there shall be a great mourning in Jerusalem . . . And one will say to him, "What are these wounds between your arms?" Then he will answer, "Those with which I was wounded in the house of my friends." (Zech. 12:10–11, 13:6 NKJV)

And then, with joy and compassion, He will gather His chosen people to Him.

Jerusalem will be the center of the universe during the millennial reign. Zechariah writes, "And it shall come to pass that everyone who is left of all the nations which came against Jerusalem shall go up from year to year to worship the King, the LORD of hosts, and to keep the Feast of Tabernacles" (14:16 NKJV).

When Jesus Christ returns to earth, He will set up His throne in Jerusalem, the city of God.

Therefore, brethren, having boldness to enter the Holiest by the blood of Jesus, . . . and having a High Priest over the house of God, let us draw near with a true heart in full assurance of faith, having our hearts sprinkled from an evil conscience and our bodies washed with pure water.
—Hebrews 10:19–22, NKJV

Day Five: Atonement Made Personal

$\mathcal{L}$et's say, for the sake of illustration, that I am a young man just starting out in the world. As I move into my first apartment, in my mailbox I find an advertisement from my local bank, promising me a loan of $20,000 to start my business.

Well, $20,000 sounds pretty good for a young man with nothing, so I go down to the bank, sign the note, and shake my banker's hand. I begin to work, but my business doesn't take off quite as I expected. And at the end of the year, when my balloon payment of $20,000 is due, I can't afford to pay off the loan.

My banker, however, is a forgiving fellow. He extends my loan for another year, but now the loan amount is $22,000, including interest. I go to work with renewed energy, striving to keep a roof above my head, meet my obligations, and put food on the table, but at the end of the year, I find I can't possibly begin to pay off my loan. My banker extends it again, with a handshake and a smile, and I find that I now owe $24,000.

Year after year I explain that I'm doing the best I can, and again, my friendly banker extends my loan. But each year my debt grows, and slowly I realize that I will never, ever be able to fulfill my obligation. It's humanly impossible.

During one visit to the bank I learn that I now owe $100,000. The bank's board of directors has decided that they

can no longer refinance my debt, and they want payment in full. Within a week.

The staggering amount is totally beyond my ability to repay. I sit down across from the banker's desk and hear the violent pounding of my heart. I'm lost, totally without hope. The bank could take everything I own, but the combined worth of all my earthly possessions wouldn't come close to paying off my debt.

Suddenly my banker leans forward and gives me a heart-rending smile. "I've been watching you," he says, folding his hands on his desk. "And you are very special to me. I will pay your debt in full. Consider yourself a free man."

I look up, unable to comprehend what would drive one man to make that kind of sacrifice for another. But as I watch, the banker pulls out his checkbook and writes a check. He takes it to the cashier and returns a moment later with my loan documents, stamped PAID IN FULL.

Unspeakable joy fills my heart, for I am free! Free from worry, from fear, from uncertainty. I have been redeemed by one who cared for me, and I can't begin to voice my gratitude for this inconceivable act of love.

My friend, love was the entire point of the Day of Atonement. The Old Testament saints saw the Messiah's act in the blood sacrifice; they placed their faith in His redeeming act in the same way that we do.

The double picture of sins covered (the sacrificial goat) and sins carried away (the scapegoat) points to Jesus and His perfect sacrifice on the cross. He covered and carried away our sins. He died for our sins and lives today interceding for us.

Thus in an impressive way, the detailed instructions concerning the sacrifices offered on the Day of Atonement

pointed to God's ultimate plan to allow His only Son to be the perfect sacrifice for sin. Until Christ came, the sins of the people were covered only temporarily. They were kept "under the cover" of the blood sacrifices for one year. After that, another sacrifice had to be offered. When Jesus died on the cross, His blood didn't just "cover" as in "hide"; it covered sin as in burying it in the deepest sea. It was over forever . . . "once for all" (Heb. 9:12 NKJV).

In this sense, Jesus' perfect sacrifice took care of the past just as it took care of the future. The people long before Jesus' death had the same opportunity to benefit from His sacrifice as we do, who live long after His death. Jesus provided a remedy for sin, for all of time. He was not only a perfect sacrifice for us, but also a perfect High Priest, continually interceding for us before the Most High God (Heb. 9:11–14, 24, 28).

We were all born into a state of sin, but God re-creates us as brand-new creatures when we place our faith in Christ. Through Jesus, God repairs the root cause of sin in us: the fact that we are sinners. Our eternal relationship with God is established. We are reconciled to our Creator. Tragically, we still sin, breaking our communion with God. But since we know Christ, we can receive forgiveness and the power to overcome the temptations we face (1 John 1:9). As we repent and confess our sins, we don't have to offer God another sin offering as the Israelites did. Instead, we appeal to the perfect offering Christ made for us once and for all.

Though the bride of Christ, the church, will be called away from the earth by the time the Antichrist appears, Yom Kippur reminds us that the church should be preaching repentance just before the Rapture. The last word Jesus Christ gave to the church was not the Great Commission. His last word to the church was *repent*.

In the first chapters of Revelation, Christ gave John the Revelator a message for seven churches of Asia. Five out of those seven churches were told to repent. I believe every detail in Scripture has a divine purpose. If five out of seven churches in Asia needed to repent, I believe five out of seven churches and five out of seven believers in America need to repent.

What is repentance? Three Greek words are used in the New Testament to indicate repentance. The first, *metamelomai*, indicates a change of mind that produces regret or remorse, but not necessarily a change of heart. I've seen many children say they're sorry for something when all they're really sorry for is the fact that they got caught. This is not true repentance.

The second word, *metanoeo*, means to change one's mind and purpose as the result of gaining knowledge. This verb, when used with the third word, *metanoia*, is true repentance. The person who truly repents has a sense of his own guilt and sinfulness, an understanding of God's mercy through Christ, an actual hatred of sin, and a desire to turn from sin and walk with God.

After committing murder and adultery, King David cried out to God for forgiveness. (See Psalm 51.) He first asked God to blot out his sin and then to wash it away. The Hebrew word for "wash" meant "to trample." In those days, women put clothes in the stream and trampled them clean with their feet. There is no English word for the Hebrew word translated "cleanse". The closest translation would be "to unsin." It means that when David stands before God, God sees him as if he had never sinned. God will say, "I find no fault in this man. He is whiter than snow."

After David's confession, the prophet told him, "The LORD also has put away your sin" (2 Sam. 12:13 NKJV). It was gone—forgiven instantly. David would continue to be open to the

word of prophecy, and as he looked into the future he saw the millennial reign of Christ and said, "Do good in Your good pleasure to Zion; Build the walls of Jerusalem" (Ps. 51:18 NKJV).

Each of us must take responsibility for our lives and stop making silly excuses. Like David, we must accept the guilty-as-charged verdict and confess our sins. God will rush to blot them out, never to remember them again.

Is there some secret sin in your life? Some practice or habit that has come between you and God? Your relationship with God is much like that with a close friend—sometimes some unspoken problem arises, and the friendship feels strained until you bring things out in the open and confess the problem.

If something lies heavily upon your conscience, take time today to confess it . . . and repent.

What can wash away my sins?
Nothing but the blood of Jesus.
What can make me whole again?
Nothing but the blood of Jesus.
Oh! Precious is the flow,
That makes me white as snow!
No other fount I know,
Nothing but the blood of Jesus.[6]
—Robert Lowry

The Feast
of Tabernacles

Day One: The Feast of Tabernacles

*T*he Feast of Tabernacles, known today as *Sukkot*, is held by divine decree on the fifteenth through twenty-first days of Tishri, September or October on the Julian calendar. The festival begins after the ingathering of the fall harvest, and is the happiest of the biblical feasts. It celebrates God's bounty in nature and God's protection, symbolized by the fragile booths in which the Israelites dwelled in the wilderness. According to Jewish belief and tradition, Sukkot also involves Gentiles, and seventy bullocks were offered up in the Temple for the seventy nations of the world (all they knew existed in that time). In the messianic age, the prophet Zechariah predicted, all nations will come up to Jerusalem to celebrate Sukkot as an affirmation of faith in God's guidance of the world (Zech. 14:16).

As seven is the number of fulfillment and completion, this seventh festival ushers in God's rest and points to the one-thousand-year Millennium, the reign of Christ.

Then the LORD spoke to Moses, saying, "Speak to the children of Israel, saying: 'The fifteenth day of this seventh month shall be the Feast of Tabernacles for seven days to the Lord. On the first day there shall be a holy convocation. You shall do no customary work on it. For seven days you shall offer an offering made by fire to the LORD. On the eighth day you shall have a holy convocation, and you shall offer an offering made by fire to the LORD. It is a sacred assembly, and you shall do no customary work on it . . . Also on the fifteenth day of the seventh month, when you have gathered in the fruit of the land, you shall keep the feast of the LORD for seven days; on the first day there shall be a sabbath-rest, and on the eighth day a sabbath-rest.

'And you shall take for yourselves on the first day the fruit of beautiful trees, branches of palm trees, the boughs of leafy trees, and willows of the brook; and you shall rejoice before the LORD your God for seven days. You shall keep it as a feast to the LORD for seven days in the year. It shall be a statute forever in your generations. You shall celebrate it in the seventh month. You shall dwell in booths for seven days. All who are native Israelites shall dwell in booths, that your generations may know that I made the children of Israel dwell in booths when I brought them out of the land of Egypt: I am the LORD your God.'" (Lev. 23:33–36, 39–43 NKJV)

The Feast of Tabernacles is also called the Feast of Lights. To commemorate the pillar of fire that led the children of Israel by night, at the end of the first day of the feast the priests and the Levites went down to the court of the women, where four huge golden candelabra had been placed on bases fifty cubits high. Each candelabrum had four branches, and each branch terminated in a huge basin in which rested a twisted wick—made of holy garments the priests had worn in the previous year. While the Levites and priests sang praises and waved torches, sixteen young men of priestly descent climbed ladders in order to pour more than seven gallons of pure oil into each basin. When the great wicks were kindled, the light from the flames was so intense that the Mishnah says there was no courtyard in Jerusalem that was not lit up with the light.[1]

How fitting that Jesus stood in the midst of His people and proclaimed, "I am the light of the world" (John 9:5 NKJV).

The Feast of Tabernacles is also called "the season of our joy." I believe Jesus was born during the time of Sukkot. He was obviously not born in December, for Luke 2:8 records that at the time of Jesus' birth there were "shepherds living out in the fields, keeping watch over their flock by night" (NKJV). From biblical times to the present, shepherds in Israel leave the cold of the open fields and pen their sheep at night beginning in the month of October. Due to the nighttime cold, there were no shepherds in any fields in December. It was customary, however, to send flocks out after Passover, and they would remain in the fields until the first rain or frost in October. Jesus' birth, then, had to occur sometime between Passover and early October. I believe He was born during the Festival of Sukkot, the season of joy!

The angels gathered on the first Christmas morning and announced, "Do not be afraid, for behold, I bring you good tidings of great joy which will be to all people" (Luke 2:10 NKJV). They knew the King of kings had come into the world. In the same way, the Feast of Sukkot celebrates the coming time when Jesus Christ will rule over the entire earth.

Zechariah prophesied that the Messiah would be God's greatest gift to the earth. "And the LORD shall be King over all the earth," he wrote. "In that day it shall be—'The LORD is one,' And His name one" (14:9 NKJV). The Messiah's coming will bring joy to the nations of the world.

Jesus Christ is our joy. As we await His second coming when He will rule over the entire world, we rejoice in the power of the name that is above every name. One of the given names of Jesus, Emmanuel, means "God with us." He is the wonderful Counselor, the mighty God, the everlasting Father, and the Prince of Peace. Our Savior and Deliverer is also our Friend and Comforter. He gives us joy today that the world will know tomorrow. In His presence is the fullness of joy.

Nearly 250 years ago, the English writer Isaac Watts wrote a hymn based on Psalm 98. Although we traditionally sing his song at Christmas, the lyrics are really about the millennial reign of Christ. How appropriate it would be to sing this song during Sukkot, the festival that points forward to the Millennium and backward to the wonderful nativity of Christ:

Joy to the world! The Lord is come;
Let earth receive her king;
Let every heart prepare Him room,
And heaven and nature sing.

He rules the world with truth and grace,
And makes the nations prove
The glories of His righteousness,
And wonders of His love.[2]
—Isaac Watts

Day Two: Tabernacles in the Time of Christ

*I*n the years after Moses taught the people about God's commandments concerning the Feast of Tabernacles, the festival degenerated into little more than a drunken party. The people did not focus upon making booths, but followed their pagan Canaanite neighbors as they celebrated the conclusion of the fall harvest—paying particular homage to the grapes from their vineyards.

Jewish scholar Hayyim Schauss writes that when the prophet Amos visited the temple at Beth-El during the autumn festival, "the revelry that he saw made such an unfavorable impression upon him that he condemned the sanctuary and the entire ritual of the festival. Hosea, who appeared as a prophet in the Kingdom of Israel a short time after Amos, also protested against the bacchanalia of the autumn festival. The same festival doubtless took place in the Kingdom of Judah, for Isaiah, who lived in Jerusalem, tells us that all, even priests and prophets, were drunk in the sanctuary."[3] (See Amos 5:21–27; Hos. 9:1; Isa. 28:7–8.)

Israel was soon sent into exile. Years later, as the people returned from their Babylonian captivity, the books of the Law were opened, read, and understood. And just as Nehemiah had Ezra read instructions about how to keep the Feast of Trumpets, Ezra also taught the people about the Feast of Tabernacles (Neh. 8:14–18).

Thus was the Feast of Tabernacles, or Booths, properly instituted. By the time of Christ, Sukkot (Hebrew for "booths") was one of the two great pilgrimage festivals. The people knew the festival by many different names: the Feast of the Ingathering (in reference to the completed harvest), the Feast of the Nations (in reference to Zechariah's prophecy that the Gentile nations would come to Jerusalem to celebrate it), and the Festival of Lights. Just as Jews from all over the world came to Jerusalem for Passover, so they came for the Feast of Tabernacles. By donkey, camel, chariot, and on foot, they traveled in huge caravans and small parties, eager to celebrate and rejoice in what God had done for them.

As they traveled along the hot and dusty roads, they sang the psalms of ascent. (See Ps. 84, for example.)

When the pilgrims reached Jerusalem, they staked out corners of the city in which to build their booths. Any available space would do—a courtyard of a house, a corner of a roof, empty lots and busy corners. Any building with an established wall was fair game, and the three-sided booths sprang up like mushrooms after a spring rain.

In comparison to the somber feasts of Rosh Hashanah and the Day of Atonement, which had just passed, the Feast of Tabernacles was a time of great joy. Not only did the temporary booths symbolize the tents in which the Israelites lived while they were divinely protected by God in the desert, but they also represented mankind's

earthly bodies, temporary dwelling places for our eternal souls and spirits.

Most of the Jews who made their way to Jerusalem during the time of the second Temple had no idea that God Himself had just *tabernacled* Himself among them. Jesus Christ, the second person of the Trinity, had stepped into a temporary tabernacle of flesh in order to bring all men to Himself. The apostle John tells us, "And the Word became flesh and dwelt among us, and we beheld His glory, the glory as of the only begotten of the Father, full of grace and truth" (John 1:14 NKJV).

Writing to a primarily Jewish audience, John used the Greek word *sk'enos* (shelter or covering) and the metaphor of a tabernacle to describe Christ's incarnation. The same word appears in Revelation 21:3, when the New Jerusalem comes down from heaven and God says, "Behold, the tabernacle of God is with men, and He will dwell with them, and they shall be His people. God Himself will be with them and be their God."

Many Bible scholars, and I count myself as one of them, believe that Jesus was born during the time of the Feast of Tabernacles. I've already mentioned the fact that it's not logical that shepherds would be outside during the month of December—the flocks were brought in to warm, sheltering caves as soon as the fall harvest was completed.

There are other indications that Jesus was born on the Feast of Tabernacles. Look at Luke 2:10. The angel appeared to the shepherds and said: "Do not be afraid, for behold, I bring you good tidings of great joy which will be to all people." The phrase "great joy" would have been automatically associated with Sukkot, for it was known as the *Season of Our Joy*. Likewise, the phrase "to all people" would remind the Jewish hearer that Sukkot was also known as the Feast of the Nations. Two strong themes of Sukkot in one short message!

Another clue that points to a Sukkot nativity is the fact that Bethlehem was so crowded there was "no room in the inn." Luke explained the crowded conditions by saying that every family had gone to their home city to be taxed, but the Romans were nothing if not logical. If you wanted to gather taxes, would you do it in the dead of winter or right after the harvest, the farmer's "payday"? Because Bethlehem is less than four miles from Jerusalem, it is logical that the little city would be crowded with pilgrims on their way to the Temple to celebrate Sukkot.

Finally, since Jesus' ministry on the cross was so vividly portrayed by the rituals surrounding Passover, Unleavened Bread, and Firstfruits, isn't it reasonable to assume that the Feast of Tabernacles illustrates His birth? The apostle John certainly thought so, for he didn't hesitate to evoke images of tabernacles to explain Christ's incarnation.

There's one other image from the Temple celebration of Sukkot that I'd like you to see. To commemorate the drawing of water from the rock at Horeb (Ex. 17:1–7), on the morning of the first day of the festival and every day thereafter, a priest carried a large golden ewer from the Temple mount down to the spring of Siloam. Surrounded by jubilant worshipers, he drew water from the pool, then returned to the Temple, walking through the water gate, which led to the inner court. A great cheering crowd waited for him near the altar. Priests blew the ceremonial silver trumpets, and other priests chanted the words of Isaiah: "Therefore with joy you will draw water From the wells of salvation" (12:3 NKJV). Don't miss the significance, my friend—""salvation" in Hebrew is *yeshua*, the same word we translate "Jesus."

On the first through the sixth days, the priest and his joyful processional circled the altar once, but on the seventh day

they circled the altar seven times! The highlight of the ceremony occurred when the priest stood and poured the water
on the altar. While the water washed away the blood of the
morning's sacrifices, a long line of priests, all bearing willow
branches, sang psalms of praise. Eddie Chumney reports that
the Talmud describes the ceremony in detail, including a portrait of venerable sages juggling lighted torches and perform-
ing somersaults as part of the celebration.[4] The experience was
one of intense and total joy, so much so that the Talmud says
whoever has not been in Jerusalem for this ceremony has not
experienced real joy![5] The water ritual, known as *Simcha Bet
Ha-sho-evah* (the Rejoicing of the House of Drawing Water)
prophetically illustrates the time when the Holy Spirit will be
poured out upon Israel.

It also illustrates the truth that Jesus Christ, the Giver of
living water, came to earth at Sukkot. Jesus told the Samaritan
woman at the well, "If you knew the gift of God, and who it is
who says to you, 'Give Me a drink,' you would have asked
Him, and He would have given you living water . . . Whoever
drinks of this water will thirst again, but whoever drinks of
the water that I shall give him will never thirst. But the water
that I shall give him will become in him a fountain of water
springing up into everlasting life" (John 4:10, 13–14 NKJV).

Like all devout Jewish men, Jesus attended the Feast of
Tabernacles in Jerusalem. On the last day of one Sukkot festival, He stood and cried out to the crowd: "If anyone thirsts, let
him come to Me and drink. He who believes in Me, as the
Scripture has said, out of his heart will flow rivers of living
water" (John 7:37–38 NKJV). The apostle John goes on to
explain that Jesus spoke about the Holy Spirit, which had not
yet been given.

Can't you just *see* it? Jesus and His disciples had just

attended the glorious celebration inside the Temple. They had sung psalms with the priests, had perhaps followed the golden ewer of water seven times around the altar. They watched the liquid stream over the altar, cleaning away the blood of goats and rams from the morning sacrifices. As the rustlings of a thousand palms filled the air, foreshadowing the palms that would be lifted to hail Him when He would enter Jerusalem to die at Passover, Jesus spoke in a commanding voice and explained the ritual the Jews had just witnessed.

He was the Light of the World, the Living Water, the Word made flesh to dwell among them. He would soon be the Passover Lamb, the Bread Without Leaven, the Firstfruits. As our sinless High Priest, He would atone for sin once and for all.

Hundreds in the Temple that day heard Him . . . but only those with understanding believed. Do you?

For I will pour water on him who is thirsty,
And floods on the dry ground;
I will pour My Spirit on your descendants,
And My blessing on your offspring.
—Isaiah 44:3 NKJV

Day Three: Present-Day Tabernacles

Contemporary Jews still consider Sukkot to be a time of great rejoicing. The festival is observed from the fifteenth of Tishri for seven days and concludes on the eighth day with the observance of *Atseret/Simchat Torah,* a service in which the congregation finishes reading the last verses of Deuteronomy and immediately begins again with the first verses of Genesis. Jewish tradition has divided the Torah into weekly portions so that one reads through the entire Torah each year. The immediate reading of the first verses of Genesis illustrates that the study of God's Word should never end.

At the conclusion of the reading, the Torah scrolls are removed from the ark in which they are kept and carried around the synagogue in a celebratory procession. Like the Jews who circled the altar in Jesus' time, the present-day celebration of Sukkot is a joyous occasion, but modern Jews credit their joy to having lived to complete the reading of the Torah yet another time so they can begin reading it again.

In some synagogues, the children are called forward at the conclusion of the service. While the adults form a canopy over them by holding their prayer shawls over their heads, the blessing of Jacob, from Genesis 49, is recited over them. As a symbol of the blessing falling upon the children of Israel, the children are given candy to remind them that the study of God's Word is sweet.

During the Feast of Tabernacles, each Jewish family participates in the building of a *sukkah,* or booth. Many families begin construction of their sukkah immediately after the conclusion of the Yom Kippur service. The booth will not be an elaborate structure. Just like the booths of Jesus' day, they may spring up almost anywhere. Sometimes apartment dwellers choose to help build a sukkah at the synagogue or at the home of friends.

The use of the *lulav* and *etrog* is an ancient practice that dates from the time of the second Temple. The lulav and etrog are also called the four species—citron, palm, myrtle, and willow. The identification of the four species is based on Leviticus 23:40: "And you shall take for yourselves on the first day the fruit of beautiful trees, branches of palm trees, the boughs of leafy trees, and willows of the brook . . ." The etrog, or citron, remains a separate entity, but the branches are bound together around one palm branch and called the lulav.

The etrog is a yellow citrus fruit about the size of a lemon, but not as sour. For generations, as the Jews celebrated the Feast of Tabernacles, they held the lulav in one hand and the etrog in the other, waving them in all four directions, north, south, east, and west.

Over the years, in an effort to understand why God commanded this ritual, the Jews have ascribed various meanings to the four species. One belief is that all four species cannot exist without water, and the Feast of Tabernacles did include prayers for rain to ensure the next year's harvest. Another idea is that the four species represent Abraham, Isaac, Jacob, and Joseph, or that they represent four classes of Jews. The first class, represented by the tasty, fragrant citron, is made up of those Jews who have knowledge of the Torah and do good deeds. The palm date has taste, but no smell, so it represents Jews who know the Torah, but do not practice good deeds. The myrtle has aroma, but no taste, so it represents Jews who perform good deeds but do not know the Torah, and the willow has neither taste nor aroma, so it portrays Jews who neither know Torah nor do good deeds.[6]

I believe, however, that the true meaning is found in the way these items are used in the Sukkot ceremony. At the beginning of the ceremony, the etrog is held upside down and in the opposite hand, but by the end of the service it is turned right side up and joined with the lulav.

I believe that the citron may represent the Gentiles who have been brought into a covenant with God through Jesus Christ. As Paul wrote in Ephesians, at one time we were "without Christ, being aliens from the commonwealth of Israel and strangers from the covenants of promise, having no hope and without God in the world. But now in Christ Jesus you who once were far off have been brought near by the blood of Christ" (2:12–13 NKJV).

During a contemporary celebration of the Feast of Tabernacles, a Jewish family will eat a holiday meal in the sukkah they have prepared. The mood is relaxed and happy, more like a picnic than a religious ritual. After blessings for wine and bread are recited, the head of the home will say a special blessing for Sukkot: "Blessed art Thou, O Lord our God, Ruler of the universe, who has set us apart by Thy commandments and commanded us to celebrate in the sukkah."

Local congregations may hold special Sukkot services on the first two nights of the festival, in which participants wave lulavs while reciting the praise psalms (Pss. 113–18). If weather permits, some families may choose to sleep in their sukkah.

The eighth day of the festival, *Shmeni Atzeret* (the Eighth Day of Assembly), is set apart as a Sabbath and a holy assembly. Why? Ask any devout Jewish parent—on the eighth day,

Jewish baby boys take the sign of the Abrahamic covenant through circumcision (Gen. 17).[7] So, too, with Jesus. Scripture tells us that when "eight days were completed for the circumcision of the Child, His name was called JESUS, the name given by the angel before He was conceived in the womb" (Luke 2:21 NKJV).

If there is one thing we can learn from the contemporary Jewish observance of Sukkot's eight-day service, it is that God's Word must be honored. How many Christians do you know who make a practice of reading the Bible through each year? How many church members would rise up and circle the sanctuary seven times while the pastor carried a copy of the Word of God in his arms?

The Word of God is worthy of our veneration, respect, and study. The Old Testament promises and prophecies are still valid and important for us to understand. Jesus said, "Do not think that I came to destroy the Law or the Prophets. I did not come to destroy but to fulfill. For assuredly, I say to you, till heaven and earth pass away, one jot or one tittle will by no means pass from the law till all is fulfilled" (Matt. 5:17–18 NKJV).

My friend, we must return our attention to the study of the Bible, God's holy Word. These treacherous times require it, our love for God compels it. May we join with the Jews during Sukkot as they say, "How sweet are Your words to my taste, Sweeter than honey to my mouth!" (Ps. 119:103 NKJV).

Hear the command of Paul: "Study to shew thyself approved unto God, a workman that needeth not to be ashamed, rightly dividing the word of truth" (2 Tim. 2:15 KJV). Now answer this question: If you read the Word of God ten minutes each day and watch television seven hours, who is Lord of your life? Hollywood or the Holy Spirit?

The law of the LORD is perfect,
converting the soul;
The testimony of the LORD is sure,
making wise the simple;
The statutes of the LORD are right,
rejoicing the heart;
The commandment of the LORD is pure,
enlightening the eyes.
—Psalm 19:7–8

Day Four: The Prophecy of Tabernacles

*W*hat is the millennial kingdom of Christ? Though it is not often preached from Sunday pulpits, the Bible has much to say about the Millennium. It is known in Scripture as "the world to come" (Heb. 2:5 NKJV); "the kingdom of heaven" (Matt. 5:10 NKJV); "the kingdom of God" (Mark 1:14 NKJV); "the last day" (John 6:40 NKJV); and "the regeneration" (Matt. 19:28 NKJV). Jesus told His disciples, "Assuredly I say to you, that in the regeneration, when the Son of Man sits on the throne of His glory, you who have followed Me will also sit on twelve thrones, judging the twelve tribes of Israel" (Matt. 19:28 NKJV).

The Millennium was foreshadowed in the Old Testament by the Sabbath, a time of rest. A rest was to be observed after six work days, six work weeks, six work months, and six work years. In God's eternal plan, the earth will rest after six thousand years as well, as He ushers in the millennial kingdom of the Messiah.

During the Millennium, the geography of Israel will be changed. Israel will be greatly enlarged and the desert will become a fertile plain. For the first time Israel will possess all the land promised to Abraham in Genesis 15:18–21. A miraculous river will flow east to west from the Mount of Olives into both the Mediterranean and the Dead Seas. But it will be "dead" no longer!

Jerusalem, the apple of God's eye, will become the joy of the world, for Jesus will reign there. The city will become the international worship center, and people from all over the world will make pilgrimages to worship in the holy Temple. Kings, queens, princes, and presidents shall come to the Holy City so "that at the name of Jesus every knee should bow, of those in heaven . . . and that every tongue should confess that Jesus Christ is Lord, to the glory of God the Father" (Phil. 2:10–11 NKJV).

The Holy City, now six miles in circumference, will occupy an elevated site and will be named *Jehovah-Shammah*, meaning "the Lord is there" (Ezek. 48:35 NKJV) and *Jehovah-Tsidkenu*, meaning "the Lord our righteousness" (Jer. 33:16 NKJV).

The Millennium will be a time of rest for the people of God. Hebrews 4:8–9 tells us, "For if Joshua [Jesus] had given them rest, then He would not afterward have spoken of another day. There remains therefore a rest for the people of God."

The prophet Isaiah echoes the thought: "And in that day there shall be a Root of Jesse, Who shall stand as a banner to the people; For the Gentiles shall seek Him, And His resting place shall be glorious" (11:10 NKJV).

Can you imagine one thousand years of perfect peace? The earth will cease from strife, and the lion shall lie down by the lamb without even showing his claws! Satan will be bound in the chambers of hell, and earthly problems will fade away. Isaiah tells us that we will also enjoy unparalleled health: "In that day the deaf shall hear the words of the book, And the eyes of the blind shall see out of obscurity and out of darkness" (29:18 NKJV).

What is the purpose of the Millennium? God has several reasons for instituting an earthly kingdom over which His Son will reign. First, He has promised to reward His children. Jesus said, "Then the King will say to those on His right hand, 'Come, you blessed of My Father, inherit the kingdom prepared for you from the foundation of the world" (Matt. 25:34 NKJV).

Second, God promised Abraham that Israel would become a mighty nation, which has already come to pass, and that his seed would someday own the promised land forever (Gen. 12:7; 13:14–17). Israel does rightfully own the land God gave to Abraham by blood covenant. When Messiah comes, the seed of Abraham will be given that land down to the last square inch.

Third, God will establish the millennial kingdom to answer a million believers' prayers. When Jesus taught His disciples the model prayer, or "the Lord's Prayer" (Luke 11:1–4), He taught them to pray, "Your kingdom come." The phrase "Your kingdom come" isn't just a little ditty meant to rhyme with "Your will be done," it is a plea that God would soon establish His earthly kingdom!

Finally, God will establish a millennial kingdom to prove a point: the Millennium will be a one-thousand-year lesson in man's ultimate depravity. The idea that man can improve himself to the point of perfection will be proved false once and for all; the concept of utopia will vanish like the morning mist. For though Christians will live in their resurrected bodies, the believers who go into the Millennium in their mortal bodies will bear children throughout the thousand years. The children and grandchildren of the Millennium will still possess a sin nature, so they will still have to choose whether or not to accept Christ as Savior.

The ages will witness one indisputable fact: Without God, man has no hope. The Bible scholar Harold Willmington illustrates it this way:

> The age of innocence ended with willful disobedience (Gen. 3).
>
> The age of conscience ended with universal corruption (Gen. 6).
>
> The age of human government ended with devil-worshiping at the Tower of Babel (Gen. 11).
>
> The age of promise ended with God's people enslaved in Egypt (Ex. 1).
>
> The age of the law ended with the creatures killing their Creator (Matt. 27).
>
> The age of the church will end with worldwide apostasy (1 Tim. 4).
>
> The age of the Millennium will end with an attempt to destroy God Himself (Rev. 20).[8]

At the end of the Millennium, Satan will be loosed from his prison, and thousands of people will follow him. A great war will be waged, and God will descend to destroy His enemies. When the battle is over, and Satan and his followers have been eternally banished to the lake of fire, God will renovate this present world.

In Revelation 20:11 John writes, "Then I saw a great white throne and Him who sat on it, from whose face the earth and the heaven fled away. And there was found no place for them" (NKJV).

The Great White Throne Judgment takes place after the millennial reign is completed. It is held in an intermediate place, somewhere between heaven and earth. It could not occur on the earth because the earth will be gone. It will not occur in heaven because sinners would never be permitted in the presence of a holy God.

> *You* may juggle human laws, you may fool with human courts, but there is a judgment to come, and from it there is no appeal.
> —ORIN PHILIP GIFFORD

In John 5:27–29, Jesus Christ says that the Father "has given Him [the Son] authority to execute judgment also, because He is the Son of Man. Do not marvel at this; for the hour is coming in which all who are in the graves will hear His voice and come forth—those who have done good, to the resurrection of life, and those who have done evil, to the resurrection of condemnation."

There are two resurrections—the resurrection of the just and that of the unjust (Acts 24:15). The resurrection of the just takes place in three phases. The first phase occurred during the Crucifixion when men came out of their graves and were seen in the city of Jerusalem. The second phase will be the rapture of the church. The third phase will be in the middle of the Tribulation, where martyred saints are taken into heaven.

As we have previously discussed, believers are judged at the bema seat of Christ. The Great White Throne Judgment is for those who have rejected Jesus Christ.

In Revelation 20:12–13 John continues to describe the Great White Throne Judgment, saying, "And I saw the dead, small and great, standing before God, and books were opened. And another book was opened, which is the Book of Life. And the dead were judged according to their works, by the things which were written in the books . . . Death and Hades delivered up the dead who were in them. And they were judged, each one according to his works."

Notice that God has two sets of books. The Book of Life contains the name of every person who accepted Jesus Christ while they were on the earth. When the wicked dead approach the Great White Throne, Jesus will first look for their names in the Book of Life. Obviously, they will not be recorded there. Then He will open the "books" that are His written records of every word, thought, and deed of the wicked. The result? "And anyone not found written in the Book of Life was cast into the lake of fire" (Rev. 20:15 NKJV).

After the Great White Throne Judgment, God will present us with a new heaven and a new earth, to which a New Jerusalem will descend from heaven (Rev. 21:9–27; 22:1–5).

Glory!

Heavenly Father, I know full well that were it not for the precious blood of Jesus, I would be standing before You at the Great White Throne. How I praise You for Your mercy! How I thank You for Your loving plan to redeem fallen men and women!

Day Five: Tabernacles Made Personal

My friend, as the days grow shorter we need to find our identity in Jesus Christ. As the Light of the World, He demonstrated who we are and what we are to be doing. Jesus urges us, "Let your light so shine before men, that they may see your good works and glorify your Father in heaven" (Matt. 5:16 NKJV). Light reveals, exposes, and finally conquers darkness. We are to be the light in a dark world, just as Christ was.

Hear this! There can be no peaceful coexistence between light and darkness. "What communion has light with darkness?" asks the apostle Paul (2 Cor. 6:14 NKJV). The time has come for the church of Jesus Christ to stop complaining about the darkness and turn on its light!

Don't whine. *Shine!*

Victory doesn't come without a fight. There is no sunrise without a night. There is no purchase without a cost. There is no crown without a cross. Don't curse the darkness, my friend, turn on the light! Spread the joy of Jesus around! I like what Billy Sunday once said: "If you have no joy in your religion, there's a leak in your Christianity somewhere."

I hope you've enjoyed this study of the biblical feasts. I want you to know that my purpose in writing this book was not to frighten or alarm you. I have intended to teach you the future through the symbolism of the seven feasts. My chief purpose in creating this book is to encourage you to live a godly life, to be a soul winner, and to prepare for the imminent return of our Lord and Savior, Jesus Christ.

God did not tell us about the future to weed out the studious from the lazy. He did not give us information about the future so we could devote the rest of our lives to figuring out the identity of the Antichrist or the precise location of Tubal. He did not give us prophecy so that we could use secret formulas to determine exactly when the Rapture would take place.

God gave us prophecy so we would know that He would win the ultimate victory, and that the world will not keep on going as it is. God gave us prophecies so that our lives might be different in light of the prophesied events. If you gain anything from this devotional book, I pray that you will appreciate the magnificent plan of God and trust in His omnipotence. The One who brought the world into being with a spoken word also has the power to create a new heaven and a new earth. He has the power to take your sin, your sicknesses, and your mortal body and give you a sinless, supernatural body.

Knowing all these things, our lives should be different. The fact that this present universe will be destroyed should spur us to holy conduct, godliness, expectant waiting for the Lord, and evangelism (2 Peter 3:11–15). Don't let yourself get bogged down in worry about our political system, the economy, your retirement plan, and the world's computer crises.

Don't let your life be controlled by anxiety and aspirin! Psalm 37 tells us to relax! God is in charge of this day, today, just as He was in charge in the days of Moses. We are commanded to delight ourselves in the Lord, and He shall give us the desires of our hearts (Ps. 37:4).

Worry is interest paid on trouble before it happens. Sometimes we worry about injustices over which we have no control. We get aggravated when evil people seem to prosper. We may even become angry with drug pushers, crooked politicians, and the powerful who laugh at and flaunt the law—while the righteous are mocked by the media and ridiculed by society as "radical, right-wing Bible believers."

We need to trust in the Lord during the dark days. Things we trust will be severely tested. We may trust in wealth, but then a recession comes. We may trust in friends, and then they betray us. We may trust in our health, and then the doctor says "cancer." Your circumstances may change, but God never changes.

When God sees His children giving praise to Him at a dark moment, He says to the angels, "Look at that one. She's praising Me even though her doctor told her about the cancer." Or, "That man just lost his job, and yet he is praising Me. Hurry, angels, take healing and comfort to them and pour out blessings they cannot contain."

If you are carrying a heavy burden, it is because you have not asked God to lighten your load. Sometimes we count blessings, but what we need to do is count our burdens, then take them to the Lord and leave them there.

I used to read "Take My yoke upon you and learn from Me" (Matt. 11:29 NKJV) and imagine myself slipping into one of those heavy wooden yokes that oxen wear as they plow the fields. In my mind's eye, I looped my arms around that yoke and trudged through the furrow, always looking ahead to the end of the row, where I imagined Jesus cheering me on. Sometimes, I'll admit, the burden grew *heavy*.

And then, one day the Spirit showed me that I had missed an important truth. Yes, Jesus said to take His yoke, but He also added, "For My yoke is easy and My burden is light" (Matt. 11:30 NKJV). Why is it light? Because Jesus isn't standing at the end of the furrow, He's walking beside you and beside me. We're not strapped into that heavy yoke alone; He walks beside us sharing, lifting the load. Anytime the yoke is too heavy, it's because we're taking all the weight ourselves. We need to give those burdens, those concerns, to Jesus. His shoulders are broader than yours and mine. If we let Him carry the weight, His yoke *is* easy, and His burden is light.

Jesus Christ, the One who tabernacled among men, knows your hurts, your longings, and secret ambitions. He understands heartache and pain. He has known betrayal. He has wept in compassion and personal loss.

And yet He will be the Victor. This present planet will dissolve away, to make way for the new heaven and new earth, where we shall live without the troubles inflicted by our sinful natures, a cursed planet, and the evil one.

Jesus is Emmanuel, God *with* us—not ahead of us, not behind us.

He is a wonderful Counselor, the mighty God, the everlasting Father, and the Prince of Peace. He is my Savior, my Friend, my Deliverer, and my Comforter.

He is the Lion of the tribe of Judah, the Alpha and the Omega, the First and the Last. The Only begotten Son of the living God is my Lord, the Friend that sticks closer than a brother.

Father, how we praise You for the example of Jesus, our living Lord. We wait expectantly for the sound of the shofar, the trumpet of God that will call us to meet Him in the air. We know the trump could sound in the next ten seconds, so help us, Father, to live this day as if it were our last opportunity to touch others with the gospel of Jesus and the love of Christ.

Notes

Week One: The Feast of Passover

1. Peter S. Knobel, ed., *Gates of the Seasons, A Guide to the Jewish Year* (New York: Central Conference of American Rabbis, 1983), 66.
2. Hayyim Schauss, *The Jewish Festivals, A Guide to Their History and Observance* (New York: Schoken Books, 1938), 46–47.
3. Mishnah, San Hedrin 97–98, quoted in Eddie Chumney's "The Seven Festivals of the Messiah," Web site: http://www.geocities.com/Heartland/2175/ chap3.html.
4. William Cowper, "There Is A Fountain," *Voice of Praise* (Nashville, TN: Broadman Press, 1947), p. 75.

Week Two: The Feast of Unleavened Bread

1. Schauss, *The Jewish Festivals,* 52.
2. Knobel, *Gates of the Seasons,* 70.
3. Alan Unterman, *Dictionary of Jewish Lore & Legend* (London: Thames and Hudson, 1991), 88.
4. Harold Willmington, *Basic Stages in the Book of Ages* (Lynchburg, VA: Harold Willmington, 1975), 369–70.
5. Story from Leviticus Rabbah 4:6 told in Rabbi Joseph Teluskin's *Jewish Wisdom* (New York: William Morrow and Company, Inc., 1994), 95.

Week Three: The Feast of Firstfruits

1. Rich Robinson, "First Fruits Then and Now," http://www.jews-for-jesus.org/Publications/newsletters/5-5757Mar97/fruits.html.
2. Schauss, *The Jewish Festivals,* 88.
3. Knobel, *Gates of the Seasons,* 131.

4. Dr. Thomas S. McCall, "The Mystery of the Date of Pentecost," Zola Levitt Ministries newsletter, July 1995.

5. Robinson, "First Fruits."

6. Walter C. Kaiser Jr., Peter H. Davids, F. F. Bruce, and Manfred T. Brauch, *Hard Sayings of the Bible* (Downers Grove, IL: InterVarsity Press, 1996), 569–70.

7. Leon Morris, *The Epistle to the Romans* (Grand Rapids, MI: Eerdmans, 1988), 323.

8. Knowles Shaw, "Bringing in the Sheaves," *Voice of Praise* (Nashville, TN: Broadman Press, 1947), 281.

Week Four: The Feast of Pentecost

1. Material adapted from Hebraic Heritage Ministries International's Web page: http://www.geocities.com/Heartland/2175/ chap6.html.

2. Schauss, *The Jewish Festivals,* 89.

3. Chart adapted from material presented by Hebraic Heritage Ministries International's Web page: http://www.geocities.com/Heartland/2175/ chap6.html.

4. Knobel, *Gates of the Seasons,* 78.

5. Schauss, *The Jewish Festivals,* 94.

6. David C. Gross, *How to Be Jewish* (New York: Hippocrene Books, 1991), 147.

7. Harold Willmington, *The King Is Coming* (Wheaton, IL: Tyndale House Publishers, 1988), 12–13.

Week Five: The Feast of Trumpets

1. Chumney, *The Seven Festivals of the Messiah,* http://www.geocities.com/Heartland/2175/ chap7.html.

2. Gayle White, "Rosh Hashana, Jewish New Year filled with ancient traditions," *Atlanta Journal Constitution*, Saturday, Sept. 19, 1998, p. D1.

3. Unterman, *Dictionary of Jewish Lore & Legend,* 168.

4. Chumney, *The Seven Festivals of the Messiah*, chap7.html.

5. Schauss, *The Jewish Festivals,* 118.

6. Schauss, *The Jewish Festivals,* 112.

7. Samuele Bacchiocchi, Ph.D., *God's Festivals in Scripture and History,* Andrews University Web page, http://www2.andrews.edu/~samuele/books/festivals_2/2.html.

8. Schauss, *The Jewish Festivals,* 147.

9. Gross, *How to Be Jewish,* 136–37.

10. Unterman, *Dictionary of Jewish Lore & Legend,* 168.

11. Knobel, *Gates of the Seasons,* p. 38.

Week Six: The Day of Atonement

1. Dwight L. Moody quoted in *The Encyclopedia of Religious Quotations,* compiled by Frank S. Mead (Old Tappan, NJ: Fleming H. Revell Company, 1965), 13.

2. John Phillips, *Exploring the World of the Jew* (Chicago: Moody Press, 1988), 92.

3. Schauss, *The Jewish Festivals,* 130.

4. Noted in two sources: Schauss, *The Jewish Festivals,* 136; and Chumney, *The Seven Festivals of the Messiah,* chap8.html.

5. Chumney, *The Seven Festivals of the Messiah,* chap.8.html.

6. Robert Lowry, "Nothing But the Blood," *Voice of Praise* (Nashville, TN: Broadman Press, 1947), 188.

Week 7: The Feast of Tabernacles

1. Mishnah, Sukkah 5:3, quoted in Chumney, "The Feast of Tabernacles" Web site http://geocities.com/ Heartland/2175/chap9.html.

2. Isaac Watts, "Joy to the World," *The Broadman Hymnal* (Nashville: Broadman Press, 1940), 137.

3. Schauss,*The Jewish Festivals,* 173.

4. Chumney, "The Feast of Tabernacles" Web site, chap9.html.

5. Barney Kasdan, "Sukkot: The Feast of Tabernacles," found at Web site http://www.umjc.org/documents/sukkot.html.

6. Schauss, *The Jewish Festivals*, 204.

7. Kasdan, "Sukkot."

8. Willmington, *The King Is Coming*, 241–42.